Pearson New International Edition

Customer Service
A Practical Approach
Elaine K. Harris
Sixth Edition

PEARSON®

Pearson Education Limited
Edinburgh Gate
Harlow
Essex CM20 2JE
England and Associated Companies throughout the world

Visit us on the World Wide Web at: www.pearsoned.co.uk

© Pearson Education Limited 2014

ISBN 10: 1-292-04035-1
ISBN 13: 978-1-292-04035-6

British Library Cataloguing-in-Publication Data
A catalogue record for this book is available from the British Library

Printed in the United States of America

Table of Contents

GLOSSARY

GLOSSARY

automatic call distribution Allows calls to be routed to the next available service provider.

automatic number identification Allows the call recipient to identify the incoming number and caller. Additional background or historical information may be displayed on the recipient's computer screen to enable him or her to better serve the customer.

brainstorming A problem-solving strategy in which groups of two or more share ideas in an open and accepting environment. Ideas are shared with the group and recorded.

"call me" Web browser Allows customers linked with a company's Internet site to be referred to a call center representative.

challenging customers Those customers with problems, questions, fears, and personalities that require us to work to achieve true communication.

churn (or churn rate) The number of customers who leave a business in a year's time divided by the number of new customers in the same period.

communication The process in which information, ideas, and understanding are shared between two (or more) people.

conflict A hostile encounter that occurs as a result of opposing needs, wishes, or ideas.

consumption behavior Refers to the customer's usage and payment patterns.

coproduction When customers participate in providing at least a part of their own customer service.

credibility The combination of our current knowledge, reputation, and professionalism.

culture The values, beliefs, and norms a group of people share.

customer attributes Characteristics that allow customers to be categorized according to demographic, psychographic, or firmographic information.

customer intelligence The process of gathering information; building a historical database; and developing an understanding of current, potential, and lapsed customers.

customer lifetime value The net present value of the profits a customer generates over the average customer life.

customer retention The continuous attempt to satisfy and keep current customers actively involved in conducting business.

customer satisfaction The customer's overall feeling of contentment with a customer interaction.

customer service Anything we do for the customer that enhances the customer experience.

customer service system Any set of procedures that contributes to the completion of customer service.

defection rate The percentage of customers who leave a business in one year.

demographic information Includes characteristics like age, income, marital status, education, stage in the family life cycle, whether they own or rent their home, gender, ZIP code, occupation, household size, mobility patterns, ethnic background, religion, and so forth.

diagramming A problem-solving strategy that involves creating a visual representation of a problem and system so that improvements may be made. Diagramming includes pro/con sheets, flowcharts, organizational charts, and mind mapping.

electronic mail (e-mail) Sending messages directly from one computer terminal to another. Messages may be sent and stored for later retrieval.

empathy The ability to understand what someone is experiencing and to take action to assist in resolving the situation.

empowerment   To enable or permit customer service providers to make a range of decisions to assist their customers.

ethics   A set of principles that governs the conduct of an individual or group.

expectations   Our personal vision of the result that will come from our experience.

external customers   The customers we do business with outside our organization.

eye contact   Allowing our eyes to make visual contact with someone else's eyes.

facsimile (FAX) machine   A machine that enables the transmission of graphic materials from one machine to another via telephone lines.

firmographic information   Includes characteristics about a company such as how many employees they have; the kind of business they are in; whether they are retail, wholesale, or a service provider; their hours of operation; and so on.

flowcharts   A diagramming approach to problem solving that charts each step of a process to assist in determining why a problem is occurring.

follow-up   Checking back to determine whether or not a situation is operating according to the initial plan.

formal leaders   Have the authority and power of their official position.

goal   An identified result to strive to accomplish.

goal setting   The process of establishing goals and evaluating their importance.

high-touch customers   Those customers who enter the customer experience expecting a high level of customer interaction.

inbound calls   Calls that originate with the customer that may include catalog ordering, billing questions, technical support, product use, or other information.

informal leaders   Have no official authority but do have the ability to influence others.

infrastructure   The networks of people, physical facilities, and information that support the production of customer service.

internal customers   The people we work with throughout our organization.

job aids   Leadership tools to reinforce training.

leadership   The ability to influence others.

listening   The ability to hear and understand what the speaker is saying.

low-touch customers   Those customers that enter the customer experience expecting a low level of customer interaction. Low touch frequently exists because of technology.

market segmentation   Dividing customers into groups with similar characteristics.

mind mapping   A creative approach to diagramming a problem in which a problem is recorded on paper and possible solutions branch out from the original problem.

mission   The means by which an organization will fulfill its purpose.

morale   An individual's or group's feelings or attitudes toward a job, supervisor, or company.

motivation   The individual drive that causes us to behave in a particular way.

needs   Our personal requirements.

negotiation   The evaluation of the possible solutions to a challenge and the selection of the solution that is mutually beneficial.

nonverbal expression   Tone and inflection of voice, facial expressions, posture, and eye contact. Nonverbal communication can contradict the message conveyed through another method of communication.

online bill paying   Offers customers the opportunity to receive and pay bills online.

organizational charts   A method of illustrating the hierarchy of a company by illustrating who reports to whom.

outbound calls   Calls that originate from the call center to the customer and are usually intended to sell products or services, conduct market research, or respond to customer inquiries.

perception   The way we see something based on our experience.

pitch   The highs and lows of the voice.

planning   Finding a recognizable direction to focus on and the establishment of specific customer service goals.

primary expectations   The customer's most basic requirements of an interaction.

problem solving   An active resolution to a challenging situation.

pro/con sheets   A simple approach to diagramming a problem that involves recording the arguments for and against a solution. .

psychographic information Focuses on lifestyle, mode of living, needs, motives, attitudes, reference groups, culture, social class, family influences, hobbies, political affiliation, and so on.

purpose The reason for an organization's existence.

reading The ability to look at and comprehend the written word.

relationship marketing Cultivating a lasting and mutually beneficial connection with customers.

reputation management The process of identifying how a company is perceived and establishing an action plan to correct, maintain, or enhance its reputation.

respect To give someone recognition or special regard.

responsibility check Assessing a situation and determining who *should* have responsibility and who really *does* have the responsibility.

scope of influence Our ability to influence others based on our perceptions or experiences.

secondary expectations Expectations based on our previous experiences that are enhancements to our primary expectations.

self-assessment An individual evaluation in which individual strengths and weaknesses are identified.

self-concept The way in which a person sees himself or herself and thinks that others see him or her.

self-sufficiency Customers using systems in place to meet their own service needs at a level that results in satisfaction.

social media Electronic communication used by consumers to share ideas, information, opinions, and personal messages.

strategy A plan for positive action.

talking Speaking, using words and terminology that others can comprehend.

teamwork Working together to improve the efficiency of the whole.

teleselling Selling products, services, or information via the telephone.

values A combination of our beliefs, perceptions, and ideas as to the appropriate response to a situation.

voice inflection A variation in the pitch, timing, or loudness of the voice.

voice mail A system in which a spoken message is recorded and stored in the recipient's voice mailbox. The recipient can later retrieve the audible message.

wants Things or experiences that are desired.

webinars Online collaboration or training.

writing Communicating by using the written word so that others can understand the intended message.

What Is Customer Service?

Remember This

A customer is the most important visitor on our premises. He is not dependent on us; we are dependent on him. He is not an interruption in our work; he is the purpose of it. He is not an outsider in our business; he is part of it. We are not doing him a favor by serving him; he is doing us a favor by giving us an opportunity to do so.

Mahatma Gandhi

CHAPTER OBJECTIVES

In this chapter, you will learn how to

- Define customer service.
- Recognize the difference between customer expectations and customer perceptions.
- List examples of customer service.
- Identify the five needs of every customer.
- Explain the difference between external and internal customers.
- Distinguish customer attributes.
- Understand the high cost of losing a customer.

Customer Service Is Important!

One of the most effective and least expensive ways to market a business is through excellent customer service. Customers are an obvious requirement for doing business. The importance of customer service is at an all-time high. Businesses are realizing that providing a product or service alone is not enough in today's competitive economic environment.

Today, customers are much more sophisticated than they were even five years ago. They are informed about how products should perform and know that if they are dissatisfied with the service they receive, someone else probably sells it and will provide greater service. They may also expect that if they express their unhappiness with a situation, a positive result will occur.

Customer service is in style! People are talking about its importance and go into the marketplace expecting to receive it. The provision of customer service is an important component of the business cycle. In many cases, customer service is the positive element that keeps current business coming back. The customer service provider is frequently the one who "saves the day" and the account.

When a person goes out of his or her way to provide excellent customer service, work is more fun and more fulfilling; as a result, positive relationships with others develop.

What Is Customer Service?

◖ **customer service**
Anything we do for the customer that enhances the customer experience.

Shockingly, the average customer service provider does not know what customer service is! **Customer service** is anything we do for the customer that enhances the customer experience. Customers have varying ideas of what they expect from customer interaction. The customer service provider must get to know his or her customers and strive to provide them with excellent customer service. No matter how accurately we see our definition of customer service, we still have to live up to what our customer thinks that customer service is. The customer's satisfaction is the goal to attain.

Examples of Customer Service

1. Receipt lookup or "return by" date on store receipts
2. Calling the customer by name
3. Easy return policy
4. Updated map of the area or Global Positioning System (GPS) in rental cars
5. A doctor calling you back to see how you are feeling after a professional visit

6. On-time delivery
7. Easy-to-use and functional web site
8. Owner's manuals and frequently asked questions online
9. Showing the customer that you care and illustrating courtesy and enthusiasm
10. Excellent follow-up
11. Empathy in handling customer complaints and questions
12. Well-explained instructions
13. Illustrations of encouragement
14. Suggesting a less expensive option
15. Accessibility when and where the customer wants it

Understanding of Satisfaction

Customer satisfaction is the customer's overall feeling of contentment with a customer interaction. Customer satisfaction recognizes the difference between customer expectations and customer perceptions. Satisfaction may develop quickly or may be cultivated over a period of time. Customers have many concerns; our job is to reduce as much of the customers' stress as possible and to create a pleasant customer experience, while also providing current information and helping to solve customers' problems. Satisfaction may be a customer's afterthought. The customer may think back on the experience and realize how pleasant or unpleasant it was.

◀ customer satisfaction
The customer's overall feeling of contentment with a customer interaction.

Why Is Excellent Customer Service So Rare?

Customer service is rare because it requires two things that the average person and organization are unwilling to commit to: spending money and taking action. In business, everyone talks about how important customer service is, but most people do not really know how to provide outstanding customer service. Customer service is much more than having a great attitude or being a people person. To prepare to provide excellent customer service, one must develop the skills to be successful.

In addition to developing skills, organizations must assess their current level of customer service and determine if it appropriately meets their current customers' needs. Customers are changing all the time. In addition to the change in people, the circumstances that customers and organizations are required to operate in may change. If customer policies were established a number of years ago or if the customer base has changed, current procedures for operation may no longer be effective. Companies must develop strategies that meet today's customers' needs and do all that they can to retain those customers.

Employees must be empowered to make decisions to benefit their customers. They must have managers who carefully hire the right people

"The absolute fundamental aim is to make money out of satisfying customers."
Sir John Egan

for the jobs and employees who are adequately trained to anticipate the challenges that may arise daily. While customer service is more than having a great attitude, it does require having the right attitude. Some people become so involved in trying to provide excellent customer service that they lose sight of the little things that the customer would appreciate.

The use of technology and current information greatly facilitates the provision of excellent customer service. We live in an age of technology in which a new and improved model is on the market almost before a new system is installed. Technology and information must work together to enhance customer service. Many up-to-date computer systems, e-mail, fax machines, printers, and messaging centers have remained unused because the information needed for their use was not developed and distributed to the appropriate customer service personnel. Customers use technology to enhance their own lives, and they expect the businesses that they work with to use it also. Sometimes the challenge is having too much information or information that is difficult to understand. Management must determine its relative importance in the total scheme of what the business is trying to accomplish. If we determine what our customer's concerns are but we do not know how to include the customer's home address, e-mail address, or other contact information in our database effectively, we may conclude that we do not have the most important information that the customer has given us.

The challenge of providing excellent customer service never ends. Individuals must periodically examine their performance to ensure that they are continuing to practice the positive skills that make providing customer service enjoyable and efficient. It is easy to slip into old behaviors when we are busy or have additional stress in our lives.

Management must periodically measure customer satisfaction. Just because an organization thinks that its customers are pleased with what the organization is doing for them does not mean that this is true. The customer must be asked questions concerning what is being done well and what could be improved. Those opportunities to express opinions must be offered in a way in which customers will actually respond to. Customers have many concerns in their lives; just because they have not complained to us does not mean that they do not have complaints or suggestions. It may mean that we have not taken the trouble to ask.

One of the best ways to become a better customer service provider is to become a better customer. As we exercise our rights as customers, we become more sensitive to and aware of what it takes to become an excellent customer service provider. What bothers each of us probably bothers our customers. Exercise your rights as a customer. Write compliment and complaint letters or e-mails to share your experiences and opinions. Fill out comment cards, and truthfully answer when someone asks how your experience was. Do not expect more of others than you do of yourself. You may learn more from your opinions than the people you are sharing them with.

Five Needs of Every Customer

Every customer comes into the customer situation with differing wants. While wants are frequently hard to identify and may occasionally be unrealistic, all customers have the following five basic needs:

1. Service: Customers expect the service that they think is appropriate for the level of purchase that they are making. A small, spontaneous purchase may have a smaller service need than a larger purchase that has been carefully planned and researched.

2. Price: The cost of everything we purchase is becoming more and more important. People and businesses want to use their financial resources as efficiently as possible. Many products previously considered unique are now considered commodities. This means that while a consumer previously had to travel to the local hamburger restaurant to purchase a hamburger, now one can be acquired at many other locations. This makes the component of price even more important to the customer.

3. Quality: Americans are less likely today to think of their purchases as throwaway items. Customers want the products that they purchase to be durable and functional until customers decide to replace them. This requirement of quality mandates that manufacturers and distributors produce products that live up to the customers' expectations of durability. Customers are much less likely to question price if they are doing business with a company that has a reputation for producing a high-quality product.

4. Action: Customers need action when a problem or question arises. Many companies offer toll-free customer assistance telephone lines, flexible return policies, and customer carryout services in response to the need for action. Customers are human beings and like to think that they are an important priority and that when a need or question arises someone will be ready and waiting to help them.

5. Appreciation: Customers need to know that we appreciate their business. Customer service providers can convey this appreciation in many appropriate ways. Saying "thank you" to the customer through our words and actions is a good starting point. Preferred customer mailing lists, informational newsletters, special discounts, courtesy, and name recognition are good beginnings to showing our customers our appreciation. Additionally, letting them know that we are glad that they have chosen to do business with us conveys a positive message. A fast-food restaurant has a sign in its drive-through lane that says, "We know that you could eat somewhere else; thank you for allowing us to serve you."

"It is impossible to satisfy your external customers over any length of time unless you also listen to and satisfy your internal customers."
John Adel Jr.

TEAM TIME

Sit down with your team (coworkers) and create your own list of five ways in which you will serve your customers. Consult the *five needs of every customer* as a starting point. Come up with one idea for each of the five needs. Price is the only one of the five needs that you may not have any influence over. Most of the other categories are needs that you can address. Be as creative as possible. After you and your team have made your list, make copies and set a time line during which everyone on your team will make their best effort to serve your customers according to the guidelines you have developed. At the end of your time line, meet again to determine if you have done a better job of serving your customers. If you have, *way to go*! If not, refine your list, set a new time line, and try it again! You will always learn from the results!

External and Internal Customers

It is important to recognize the importance of both external and internal customers because both contribute to the customer service of our organization. **External customers** are the customers we do business with outside our organization. External customers are the customers we most commonly think of when we consider whom we serve. They are the people with whom we interact and share our knowledge and positive attitude. External customers have the power to enhance our reputation and to bring us new business, but they are not the only customers that we serve.

Every day we interact with a special group of customers who frequently go unrecognized. These customers are our internal customers. Our **internal customers** are the people we work with throughout our organization. They are important to our success in providing our external customers with what they need. If internal customers do not see the importance of completing work promptly and of treating others with respect, it becomes very difficult for the organization to provide outstanding customer service to external customers. Internal customers were previously referred to as "coworkers," but this title does not elicit the respect deserved by the people within any organization who contribute to the overall success of the organization. Your customers may get a paycheck from the same company that you do.

The idea that all of us have customers does not appeal to those employees who want to think that because they do not interact with external customers they do not have a responsibility in the customer process. Our internal customers should be as important to us as our external customers.

external customers
The customers we do business with outside our organization.

internal customers
The people we work with throughout our organization.

By developing positive relationships with our internal customers, we are showing them that we value their importance in the overall organization. We can apply a slightly modified version of the Golden Rule to our internal customers, "Do unto our internal customers as we would do unto ourselves." This rule suggests that as customer service providers we will strive to determine what our internal customers' needs and expectations are and place the same level of importance on their needs as we would place on our own. We must stop and ask them what we can do to make their jobs easier, and they have to ask us the same thing. Working with our internal customers is not a form of manipulation but, instead, a positive approach to being part of a team. All of the team members are working together to win, but not all are making the same type of contribution.

Management has an important role in creating an environment that recognizes the importance of internal customers. By providing opportunities for internal customers to experience the challenges of each other's responsibilities, an increased respect can develop. It also helps everyone involved to see the big picture. It is a natural human tendency to assume that someone else has an easier job and an easier life than we have. Obviously, this is not necessarily the case. By beginning to understand our coworkers' challenges, we can work to minimize them. Systems may be redesigned, paperwork may be reduced, and a team approach may emerge.

By satisfying our internal customers, we create an excellent foundation on which to begin meeting our external customers' needs. Fewer apologies have to be made, work gets done more efficiently, and an overall positive atmosphere develops. If you cannot quite decide who your internal customers are, think of it this way, "Whose out-box do you work from and whose in-box do you feed into?" In addition, consider who cleans the building, who does your typing, who maintains your security, who makes the sales, and who works on the computers. These are your internal customers. A team with the goal of providing excellent customer service to all customers may make a common vision of customer service a reality with real opportunities.

Job Link

Write down the names of two key *external* customers and two key *internal* customers. For one week, call each by name when you interact with them and do all that you can to serve them completely. At the end of the week, assess your relationship with each of them. Do they perceive (in your opinion) that they have received a higher level of service from you? How do you feel about them?

Customer Attributes

customer attributes Characteristics that allow customers to be categorized according to demographic, psychographic, or firmographic information.

Each customer is, of course, unique. Identifying customer attributes may allow an organization to better understand "who" its customers are. **Customer attributes** are characteristics that allow customers to be categorized according to demographic, psychographic, or firmographic information. Businesses frequently attempt to group their customers to enable the business to serve customers more appropriately. **Demographic information** includes characteristics like age, income, marital status, education, stage in the family life cycle, home ownership, sex, ZIP code, occupation, household size, mobility patterns, ethnic background, and religion. Demographic information is a straightforward and basic method of identifying customers.

demographic information Characteristics like age, income, marital status, education, stage in the family life cycle, home ownership, sex, ZIP code, occupation, household size, mobility patterns, ethnic background, and religion.

Psychographic information focuses on lifestyles, modes of living, needs, motives, attitudes, reference groups, culture, social class, family influences, hobbies, political affiliation, and so on. Psychographic information can provide a more thorough picture of the customer. Not all individuals who earn the same income choose to spend it in the same way. Just because people live next door to you does not mean that they choose to maintain their home like yours or that they share your hobbies.

Firmographic information includes characteristics about a company such as how many employees they have; the kind of business they are in; whether they are retail, wholesale, or a service provider; their hours of operation; and so on. Since so many customer service providers serve the business-to-business environment, it has become increasingly important to understand companies themselves as entities rather than just the individuals served as the ultimate (or end-of-the-line) consumers. Individuals take their personal experiences with them as they make business decisions and vice versa.

psychographic information Lifestyles, modes of living, needs, motives, attitudes, reference groups, culture, social class, family influences, hobbies, political affiliation, and so on.

Cost of Losing a Customer

firmographic information Characteristics about a company such as how many employees they have; the kind of business they are in; whether they are retail, wholesale, or a service provider; their hours of operation; and so on.

Because of the increased expectations of customers and the competitiveness of the marketplace, customer service providers are recognizing the high cost of losing customers. It takes little effort to lose a customer. When service providers neglect their concerns, treat them disrespectfully, and fail to follow through with results, customers will be tempted to make their exit.

When customers cease to do business with us and begin to do business with our competition, several unfortunate situations occur.

- A first situation is where we lose the *current dollars* that our business relationship created. This loss may seem insignificant to begin with, but over a period of time it can prove to be quite damaging.

- A second situation is that we lose the *jobs* that our client or clients provide. If business goes elsewhere, we do not need to employ the people who were working on the account or accounts. An advertising agency lost a major advertising account because of a lack of courtesy and follow-through on the agency's part. This loss of business resulted in the closing of the office, with over 50 people suddenly out of work.
- A third situation that may occur is the *loss of reputation.* Word travels fast in our information-based society. Our clients will possibly share their experiences with their clients and friends. This loss may result in the immediate departure of other business or simply in a lack of trust among our current clients and any potential customers.
- A final challenge is the *loss of future business.* This is an intangible variable because it is difficult to assess the long-term effects of what might have happened in the future. Nevertheless, whether it is one dollar or a million, its importance is worth recognizing.

KEY TERMS

customer attributes

customer satisfaction

customer service

demographic information

external customers

firmographic information

internal customers

psychographic information

QUICK QUIZ

1. Customer service is anything we do for the customer that enhances the customer's experience. T or F
2. Customer service and satisfaction are easy to measure. T or F
3. Customer service requires nothing more than a positive attitude. T or F
4. Compliment letters can help to reinforce excellence in customer service. T or F
5. Technology can be used to enhance the provision of customer service. T or F
6. Service, price, quality, action, and appreciation are referred to as the five needs of every customer. T or F
7. The people we work with outside our organization are called internal customers. T or F
8. Customer attributes are characteristics that allow customers to be categorized. T or F
9. Information that focuses on lifestyles, modes of living, needs, motives, attitudes, and so on are referred to as demographic information. T or F
10. The losses of dollars, jobs, reputation, and future business are consequences of losing customers. T or F

OPPORTUNITIES FOR CRITICAL THINKING

1. What is the definition of customer service?
2. List five examples of customer service.
3. What are the five needs that every customer has?
4. Explain why it is necessary for customer service providers to maintain a positive relationship with both internal and external customers.
5. How is technology enhancing the provision of excellent customer service?
6. Relate customers' expectations about price to their expectations of service.
7. Is the loss of current dollars the only concern when a customer is lost?
8. List ways in which you can become a better customer.
9. Write your own philosophy and definition of customer service.
10. Define contentment.

SKILL BUILDING

My Customer

Excellent customer service providers are continually assessing their own performance and the needs of their customers. The benefits of knowing our customers include enhanced service opportunities and an awareness of service weaknesses.

Individually, or in a small group, answer the following questions:

- *My customer* is satisfied when …
- *My customer* would like for me and my organization to improve our service by …
- I anticipate *my customer's* needs by …

- The most basic customer service action that I can take for *my customer* is …
- The greatest demands on me and my time are …

Ethics in Action

A group of your coworkers goes to lunch several times a week. Although the time together usually starts out positive it frequently disintegrates into a trash talk session with your boss as the center of the conversation. You like your boss, although he can be quirky, and really like your job. What do you do?

CHALLENGE

Writing Compliment and Complaint Letters (or e-mails)

There are many ways of beginning the process necessary to become a better customer. An effective method for exercising your rights as a customer is to write compliment and complaint letters.

Many customer concerns are not effectively addressed when they occur, and the customer continues to feel anger or frustration over the situation. By taking the initiative to express customer concerns or satisfaction, a customer may feel closure in a given situation and has shared critical information with the organization.

When writing a complimentary letter, it is important to include as many facts as possible. Unfortunately, most customers are much more interested in expressing their dissatisfaction than their satisfaction. By writing a complimentary letter, you are giving an employee, department, or company a pat on the back that affirms for them that they are doing an effective job of meeting their customers' needs. Verify the accuracy of the address or e-mail address that you are using for your communication. A compliment or complaint letter or e-mail accomplishes nothing if it doesn't go to the proper place or person.

What to Include in a Complimentary Letter

- Your name, address, home and work telephone numbers, e-mail address, and account number, if appropriate.
- Make the letter brief and to the point. Share specific facts about the situation, including the name of the individual(s) that assisted you, the date of the interaction, and what pleased you.
- Type your letter if possible; it will look more professional and will be easier to read.
- Always keep a copy of any correspondence that you send. You may want it for future reference or to use as a sample for another complimentary letter in the future. If your compliment is sent in e-mail form, always send yourself a copy. This way you know that the communication went through and it will be saved on your computer in an additional form.
- Following is a guide to writing an effective compliment letter.

As with a complimentary letter, when writing a complaint letter, it is important to include specific facts. Complaint letters should be to the point and nonemotional. Complaint letters provide the writer with the opportunity to express concerns, document grievances, and to request specific or nonspecific resolutions to the situation.

Sample Compliment Letter

> (Your address)
> (Your city, state, ZIP code)
> (Date)
>
> (Name of contact person)
> (Title)
> (Company name)
> (Street address)
> (City, state, ZIP code)
>
> Dear (contact person):
>
> I would like to express to you how pleased I was with my recent interaction with your company. On (date), I called your customer service department to request assistance with my account. I was connected with (name). After patiently listening to my problem, she (he) explained very clearly what had transpired and that I had, in fact, been billed properly. (Name's) professional approach and excellent communication skills allowed me to become better informed as to how your company works and went a long way in confirming my loyalty to your organization.
>
> Thank you for providing me with such a positive customer experience.
>
> Sincerely,
>
> (Your name)
> (Office and home phone numbers with area code)
> (Your account number)

What to Include in a Complaint Letter

◾ Your name, address, home and work telephone numbers, and account number, if appropriate.

◾ Make your letter brief and to the point. Detail specific facts about the situation. Include the date and place of the purchase and information about the product or service.

◾ State exactly how you would like to see the situation resolved and when you expect to see the resolution in effect.

◾ Type your letter if possible and include copies of all pertinent documents. Do not send originals; retain them along with a copy of your correspondence for future reference. Remember, if you are expressing your complaint via e-mail, send yourself a copy.

The following sample complaint letter provides a guide to writing an effective complaint letter.

Sample Complaint Letter

> (Your address)
> (Your city, state, ZIP code)
> (Date)
>
> (Name of contact person)
> (Title)
> (Company name)
> (Street address)
> (City, state, ZIP code)
>
> Dear (contact person):
>
> On (date), I bought (or had repaired) a (name of product with serial or model number or service performed). I made this purchase at (location, date, and other important details of the transaction).
>
> Unfortunately, your product (or service) has not performed well (or the service was inadequate) because (state the problem).
>
> Therefore, to resolve the problem, I would appreciate you (state the specification you want). Enclosed are copies (copies—not originals) of my records (receipts, guarantees, warranties, canceled checks, contracts, model and serial numbers, and any other documents).
>
> I look forward to your reply and a resolution to my problem and will wait (set time limit) before seeking third-party assistance. Please contact me at the above address or by phone at the numbers shown below.
>
> Sincerely,
>
> (Your name)
> (Office and home phone numbers with area code)
> (Your account number)
>
> Enclosures
> *Source*: Southwestern Bell Telephone Book, 1992–1993.

Challenge Objectives

1. To demonstrate the ability to express both a positive and negative customer service experience in print.
2. To explore the possibility of a corporate response to written communication.
3. To refine individual business communication skills.

Assignment

Compose two letters explaining two separate customer service experiences that you have had or someone close to you has had. One letter should explain a positive experience and should show appreciation for those who offered the positive treatment. The second letter should express your dissatisfaction over a poor customer service experience. Try to include as many details as you can, including specific names, dates, and so on. You may wish to ask for some type of follow-up if you feel that it would be appropriate in the situation. You are the judge as to whether the situation is worthy of your correspondence.

Presentation

All professional business correspondence should be typed on a computer. Follow the guidelines for writing a compliment/complaint letter. Always remember to include your full name and address so that the business will know whom to send a response to. Be specific when describing what you would like to see happen in response to your letter. Always keep a copy of anything that you mail or e-mail. You will have it to refer to in the future and can use it as an example when writing your next compliment/complaint letter. Most important, mail your letters! Record on your calendar when the letters were sent and watch the mail for a reply. Happy writing!

Helpful hint: Many word-processing programs have letter wizards to assist you in writing professional letters. If you have limited experience with writing business letters, you may want to give one a try.

ANSWERS TO QUICK QUIZ

1. T	5. T	9. F
2. F	6. T	10. T
3. F	7. F	
4. T	8. T	

The Challenges of Customer Service

The Challenges of Customer Service

Remember This

A reputation once broken may possibly be repaired, but the world will always keep its eyes on the spot where the crack was.

Joseph Hall

CHAPTER OBJECTIVES

In this chapter, you will learn how to

- Identify common barriers to customer service.
- Recognize and manage customer perceptions.
- Assess primary and secondary expectations.
- Define scope of influence and determine ways to use it to maximize the perception of customer service.

- Explain tips for cultivating credibility.
- List and interpret the ethics checklist.

Elements of Success

Customer service is such a valuable concept that it seems it would be simple to provide it. Unfortunately, this is not necessarily the case. After assessing their own strengths and weaknesses, customer service providers must begin to understand the customers that they are serving. After doing this, they may begin to be prepared to provide those customers with excellent customer service. By becoming familiar with the various barriers to customer service, recognizing the power of perceptions, understanding expectations, and maintaining their own credibility and sense of values, customer service providers are equipping themselves to fully serve their customers.

Barriers to Excellent Customer Service

Numerous obstacles stand in the way of the delivery of excellent customer service. Some of the common barriers include management philosophy, difficulty for customers with a problem to contact a company or the person who can really help, unreliable equipment, restrictive company policies, difficult-to-understand warranties or owners' manuals, out-of-date procedures, and a lack of understanding of the value of service. These barriers are, in most cases, beyond the control of the customer service provider and, unfortunately, a common part of doing the job.

"The function of the customer service department is to be an advocate for the customer."
Jonathon P. Harris

Some barriers to excellent customer service are within the control of the customer service provider. These challenges can be overcome through diligent effort, allowing the customer service provider to do the best possible job. Some of the most common barriers to excellent customer service are

1. Laziness
2. Poor communication skills
3. Poor time management
4. Attitude
5. Moodiness
6. Lack of adequate training
7. Inability to handle stress
8. Insufficient authority
9. Serving customers on autopilot
10. Inadequate staffing

Customer service providers must perform periodic self-evaluations to assess their effectiveness and to identify areas that need improvement. When that assessment is made, the individuals must take the initiative to make changes and must monitor themselves so that they do not slip into their old habits.

Power of Perceptions

When we interact with others, we must be aware of their perceptions of situations, experiences, and people. A **perception** is the way that we see something based on our experience. Everyone's perception of a situation will be, at least slightly, different. The question persists, "Is the glass half full or is it half empty?"

Perceptions are frequently developed over a period of time and reflect the ways that we have been treated, our values, priorities, prejudices, and sensitivity to others. Two people can share the same experience and then describe it differently. Unfortunately, perceptions are not necessarily based on rational ideas and may be influenced by momentary frustration and anger. Because perceptions are so full of mystery, it is important for the customer service provider to anticipate customer resistance based on the customers' prior interactions and always to work at providing the customers with excellent service so that their most current perception is a positive one. Customers may not remember every detail of an experience, but they will retain an overall feeling about it. That "feeling," in combination with other experiences, will create their perception of your company and you.

Whenever possible, try to deal with your customers as individual human beings. Respect their time, circumstances, and priorities. Always convey to customers that you appreciate the time it takes them to do business with your company. Ask the customers if there is anything else that you can do for them. Periodically, ask the customers how you are doing. The feedback that they give you will provide insights as to how they perceive your organization. Remember that you may not be able to erase customers' negative perceptions that are based on their prior interactions. What you can do is to show them, through your actions, that their perceptions are not accurate.

Understanding Expectations

Every customer walks into a known or unknown situation with a set of expectations. **Expectations** are our personal vision of the result that will come from our experience. Expectations may be positive or negative. How many times have you practiced your response to an anticipated objection only to find out that you did not have to use it? Expectations are usually based, at least partially, on our perceptions. If your last experience with a company was negative, you may approach a new situation with the expectation that you will again be dissatisfied. Because of this, you may approach the interaction "armed and ready" for battle.

Sometimes companies or individuals wrongly assume that they cannot live up to their customers' expectations. This assumption frequently stems from a misconception of what the customers expect.

At an educational institution, school representatives and students were informally surveyed to determine the students' expectations of the institution. The results showed a broad disparity between what the students expected and what the school representatives thought the students expected. The representatives of the school ranked the students' top five expectations of the school as follows:

1. Grades with no effort
2. Extra assistance with enrollment
3. Short classes
4. No reading assignments
5. More parking

The students ranked their own expectations this way:

1. Positive environment that encouraged learning
2. Transferable classes
3. Instructors who cared and knew the students' names
4. Safety in the parking lot and building
5. More parking

It is easy to identify the differences between the two lists. It would be incorrect to assume that all students shared the surveyed students' expectations. It would also be incorrect to assume that there were not some students who did have the expectations that the school representatives perceived that they had.

What is important to learn from this comparison is that what our customers expect is frequently much easier and less costly to provide than we may think. What the students expected cost relatively little or nothing to provide; but, because the school did not understand the students' expectations, they were not being consistently fulfilled.

Levels of Expectations

Customer service providers must recognize that customers have different levels of expectations. Expectations can be divided into two distinct categories: primary expectations and secondary expectations.

are the customers' most basic requirements of an interaction. When dining at a restaurant, our primary expectations are to satisfy our hunger, to let someone else do the cooking, and to pay a reasonable price.**Primary expectations**

Secondary expectations are expectations based on our previous experiences that are enhancements to our primary expectations. When dining at a restaurant, our secondary expectations are to have good service; to be treated with courtesy; and to receive good, tasty food.

primary expectations
The customers' most basic requirements of an interaction.

secondary expectations
Expectations based on our previous experiences that are enhancements to our primary expectations.

23

A customer's expectations change constantly, and each customer will have his or her own unique set of expectations. While this is a challenging reality, it provides a unique opportunity for us to strive consistently to be what the customers want us to be.

Scope of Influence

It is important for businesses to recognize the influence that their customers have on other customers and potential customers. This is called scope of influence. **Scope of influence** is our ability to influence others based on our perceptions or experiences. Each person's "scope" is different. On average, our opinions influence between seven and fifteen people. Some people have a larger scope because they interact with a larger number of people or because they have outgoing, open personalities.

Scope of influence plays no favorites and is usually not objective. Thus, it is extremely important to do all we can to make our customers happy and to keep their business. Studies have shown that it costs about five times as much to attract new customers as it costs to keep our current customers. Research has also shown that customers are more likely to share a negative experience with their superiors. These superiors are frequently the people with more decision-making power, income, and influence. Unfortunately, customers are likely to share a positive experience with the people closest to them and with no one else. Additionally, with the growth of digital cameras, camera phones, and the Internet as communication tools, a negative message can be easily shared with the masses with minimal effort.

The overwhelming popularity of Facebook has impacted the reality of scope of influence in an enormous way. Good or bad information is shared with the click of a button. Rarely is negative or inaccurate information retracted to the degree that it would undo damage to an individual or business's reputation. On the other hand, Facebook can be used as an effective means to get a message out quickly and to a large number of people. At the close of a recent semester, students at the University of Oklahoma announced via Facebook that a "Silent Rave" would be held at a designated time at the campus library. Although the information was shared only for a day, several hundred students showed up and participated in the activity. Organizers considered it a success and were amazed that Facebook was so effective in getting the word out so quickly and to so many people.

Marketing professionals have long recognized the power of word-of-mouth advertising. This is basically what scope of influence is. We must ask, remind, and entice our customers to share their positive experiences with others. By doing so, we are showing our current customers how much we appreciate them and we are also creating an opportunity for new customers to come to us expecting a positive experience. A happy customer can attract new customers at virtually no cost.

Job Link

Write down the names of *four people* on whom you have a lot or a little influence. Now write down the names of *as many people as you can think of* on whom each of them has an influence. Remember, family, friends, coworkers, neighbors, and so on are all in our scope of influence. You probably have a long list of names. Think of the opportunity for influence that the names on that list have (and all of the names you forgot) the next time that you are serving a customer.

Reputation Management

One way that some companies are trying to differentiate themselves from the competition is through reputation management. **Reputation management** is the process of identifying how a company is perceived and establishing an action plan to correct, maintain, or enhance the company's reputation. As more and more products and services become commodities, customers may be attracted to a company more because of its reputation than because of any other single factor. Reputation management moves away from how a company would like to be perceived and identifies and responds to how it really is perceived. A good reputation is cultivated over time through a company, department, or individual's performance, good or bad, in a variety of situations.

A company seeking to begin to manage its reputation must survey its customers and the community at large to assess what its reputation really is. A company's reputation is different from its image. A company could have a positive image but not a positive reputation. A company may be recognized as a positive and likable member of the community, but customers may still consistently decide to do business elsewhere.

A company with a good reputation

- Is trustworthy
- Demonstrates excellence in its management at all levels
- Is law abiding
- Is responsive
- Follows through on promises and commitments
- Is ethically responsible
- Is a positive public citizen
- Has accurate and strong financials
- Communicates effectively
- Shows ongoing positive social responsibility

reputation management The process of identifying how a company is perceived and establishing an action plan to correct, maintain, or enhance the company's reputation.

> *"The reputation of a thousand years may be determined by the conduct of one hour."*
> Japanese proverb

By effectively managing its reputation, a company can maintain an informed and realistic understanding of how customers and the community perceive it, which can help it to anticipate and plan for challenges in the future.

Techniques for Exceeding Customers' Expectations

To begin attempting to exceed customers' expectations, try the following:

1. **Become familiar with your customers:** Get to know who they are and why they do business with you. Find out their likes and dislikes.
2. **Ask your customers what their expectations are:** Find out what they see as the benefit of doing business with you. What would they like for you to do that you are not already doing?
3. **Tell your customers what they can expect:** Convey to your customers your commitment to them.
4. **Live up to their expectations:** Follow through by accomplishing what you have said that you would do.
5. **Maintain consistency:** Do not promise what you cannot deliver, but always deliver a consistent service. Customers like to know that they will have the same positive experience every time they interact with you.
6. **Communicate with customers using the method they want to use:** If customers prefer face-to-face communication, provide that; if they prefer online ordering or assistance, provide that; etc.

One important key to exceeding customers' expectations is to remember that expectations are always changing. What was previously in excess of our customers' expectations may suddenly be no different from what all of our competition is doing. If we fail to stay current with our competition, we may fail to live up to our customers' current expectations.

The American auto industry was for many years the world standard for excellence in automobiles. With many loyal customers, its position in the marketplace seemed secure. It had set the standard of excellence. At the same time, foreign automakers were watching and observing what customers appeared to like and to dislike. The Americans paid little attention to this potential competition; after all, they had set the standard. Suddenly, seemingly out of nowhere, a new group of competitors had entered the marketplace. These new competitors knew what customers liked and disliked about American cars. The American auto industry was shocked; how could its customers turn their backs and purchase automobiles from non-American manufacturers?

Unfortunately, what the American automakers failed to remember is that once a standard is set, it represents an opportunity for the competition to attempt to surpass it. No industry has ever continued to maintain a loyal customer base without continuously recognizing what the competition is doing and continuing to meet the customers' ever-changing needs and wants and practicing continuous improvement. Fortunately, the American auto industry has recognized what the competition is doing and has regained many of the customers that it had lost. The American automotive industry is continuing to face new challenges, but understanding their customers will be a positive part of their recovery.

Keys to Credibility

In all aspects of our lives, we are confronted with the challenge of being believable to those around us. How believable we are, in combination with how reliable we are, translates into how credible we are to others. **Credibility** is made up of the combination of our current knowledge, reputation, and professionalism. Credibility encourages trust. If we are to work successfully with our customers, they must trust us. Our personal credibility can be the one characteristic that determines our success as people and as customer service providers.

Try these tips for cultivating credibility:

1. **Practice consistency:** Approach similar situations in the same manner, always striving for fairness. Demonstrate your emotional stability. Be positive, professional, and warm at all times.
2. **Keep your word:** Follow through with the commitments that you make. Any call you receive expresses the implication that you will respond with answers. People will not have faith in you if you break your promises.
3. **Develop your expertise:** Become very knowledgeable about your products, your company, and the overall industry. Strive for continuous improvement.
4. **Become a teammate with your coworkers:** Working successfully with others shows that you have common goals and can benefit from each individual's specific skills.
5. **Show your dedication to customers:** Tell customers what you will do for them, take every request seriously, and follow up.
6. **Treat all of your customers and coworkers with the same high level of respect:** By showing that you respect others, you create an

credibility Made up of the combination of our current knowledge, reputation, and professionalism.

environment that allows others to respect you. Be sensitive to your effect on customers.

7. **Apologize if you are wrong:** Your honesty will impress others and they will respect you for who you are, not who you pretend to be.
8. **Remember that credibility is much harder to regain than it is to keep.**

Importance of Values

values A combination of our beliefs, perceptions, and ideas about the appropriate response to a situation.

For excellent customer service to exist, the successful joining of corporate values and employee values has to occur. **Values** are a combination of our beliefs, perceptions, and ideas about the appropriate response to a situation. Both individuals and companies have their own specific sets of values. Companies must effectively communicate to their employees what the company's values are. Stated corporate values are most commonly conveyed to employees through written information in employee manuals or policy statements. Real corporate values can also be conveyed through the actions of the management in an organization. Employees must recognize their own values and beliefs and attempt to identify organizations that have similar priorities.

Individual values are very personal. No other person has had the same set of circumstances that have allowed you to develop the values that you possess. In the customer service industry, some organizations have a very distinct set of dos and don'ts. Other organizations may be more vague in expressing corporate priorities to employees. In either instance, the customer service providers must recognize that they are both representatives of their company and individuals. Their behaviors and philosophies illustrate the people they are.

TEAM TIME

Sit down with your team and discuss the concept of credibility. Remember, *credibility is made up of the combination of our current knowledge, reputation, and professionalism.* Each member of your team should evaluate the credibility of your group and his or her own credibility. Choose one of the tips for cultivating credibility and create an action plan to increase the credibility of the group. Independently create your own action plan to increase your personal credibility. Set a time line to evaluate your progress as you work toward increasing the credibility of your team. As you work toward achieving your goal, do not forget that *credibility is much harder to regain than it is to keep.*

Ethics in Customer Service

Most individuals are periodically faced with ethically challenging situations. What exactly are ethics and why do they matter in our professional and personal lives? **Ethics** are a set of principles that govern the conduct of an individual or group. Sometimes ethical decisions are easy to recognize and are perceived as popular choices of behavior by the people around us. At other times, the spectrum of potential choices falls into gray areas in which the "right" or "wrong" course of action is difficult or nearly impossible to identify. The challenge of ethical decision making becomes even harder when it is not just an individual's personal judgment that is involved but also carrying out the instructions of a supervisor; request of a customer; policy of the organization; or some other situation in which a threat, real or perceived, is involved.

ethics A set of principles that govern the conduct of an individual or group.

There are really no shortcuts when it comes to telling the truth and determining an appropriate course of action. Individuals in business must be seen by those around them as honest or they will not succeed for long. The bottom line in decision making is that individuals must face the consequences of their decisions—good or bad. When faced with an ethically challenging situation, ask yourself the following questions:

- Is it legal?
- Is it fair?
- How do I feel about it?
- Would the court of public opinion find my behavior incorrect?
- Am I fearful of what those I trust would say about my actions?

These questions can be quite revealing when attempting to choose an ethical course of action. This is not to suggest that ethically challenging situations are easily resolved, but analyzing a situation may make the appropriate decision easier to identify. One final consideration regarding ethical behavior is that it is not always popular to "do the right thing," but maintaining individual integrity and an organization's reputation will allow all involved to know that they examined all possibilities and chose the most appropriate course of action.

Current Status of Customer Service

Although everyone talks about how important customer service is, they often do very little to improve it. This can be attributed to several causes.

1. It is frequently difficult to measure the financial benefits of customer service. It may be challenging to convince some financial managers of the long-term payoffs.

2. Customers have high expectations of what they hope to gain from the people with whom they do business, but frequently customer service providers do not know what those expectations are.

3. Customers have grown accustomed to expecting improved levels of customer service and considerable latitude when it comes to receiving customer service, but the resulting cost is becoming prohibitive for many businesses. Frequently, the customers who take advantage of customer-friendly policies are abusing the opportunity and represent minimal percentages of the overall business. Businesses now have to retrain customers about appropriate and realistic expectations.

4. Technology provides the opportunity for faster responses to customer questions, but it also creates the requirement that customer service providers have additional training to become proficient in using new systems.

5. Customer service is an opportunity that no professional can afford to ignore. It is frequently the distinguishing difference between two or more companies that offer the same product or service.

"The next mile is the only one a person really has to make."

Danish proverb

New Trends in Customer Service

Several new trends are emerging in the customer service industry. These trends reflect the ways in which customers approach a business interaction and the ways that businesses are preparing to respond to them. The trends include accessibility for the customer, immediacy of response, feedback from customer to customer service provider, outsourcing of all or part of customer service functions, increasing use of technology to provide all levels of service, and nontraditional examples of customer service.

Customers today have more access to information about their account status, billing, delivery, and product availability than ever before. This accessibility has, in many cases, reduced the questions that customer service providers must respond to, leaving them to respond to more unique requests. An example of this accessibility is found in customer information hot lines that can be reached from a touch-tone telephone using personal identification numbers; a second example is computer software that tracks where a shipment is, whether the shipment has been received, and by whom, finally any online means of customer contact. This includes customers serving themselves or requesting information or follow-up from a customer service provider. Customers appreciate the control that this accessibility allows them, and it reduces the number of routine questions that customer service providers must answer. It is also a wonderful illustration of technology at work.

Immediacy of response is another trend in customer service. Again, with technology, customers can have questions or problems resolved almost immediately. Customer service providers are also more fully empowered to make decisions in response to customer inquiries that previously would have been taken to a higher level supervisor.

Feedback is important to all businesses and can provide opportunities for growth in the customer service department. Customer suggestions are now frequently requested and encouraged. Independent research departments or companies to survey customer responses may contact customers. Numerous reward or preferred customer programs track customer purchases and customer preferences and can customize the customer's service experience from the swipe of a barcode that the customer provides. Customer service providers are also beginning to keep logs of customer suggestions and requests so that improvements can be made efficiently. Customers appreciate the chance to share their ideas and to see changes being made.

As businesses seek new strategies to improve performance, save money, and effectively address increasingly technical requests, outsourcing may be an effective alternative. Competition has forced many industries to begin outsourcing such functions as payroll, data processing, billing, maintenance, marketing, accounts receivable, and many more. The specialized customer service needs of many businesses are also being outsourced. Outsourcing can provide cost savings in rent, benefits, equipment, and short-term employee expense, and it can also allow organizations of all sizes to better serve their customers. Most organizations receive customer questions, complaints, and comments via 800 numbers, e-mail, and through customer surveys. While this allows closer interaction with customers, it has also decreased the expected response time. The necessary equipment to receive and respond to these contacts is costly; when added to the cost of hiring and training effective customer service representatives, some organizations may find that they cannot afford to provide this service. By hiring a carefully chosen outside company to handle specialized technical questions, customer concerns, and product inquiries, companies can decrease customer response time and share the cost of providing the service among participating companies. The most positive potential benefit is increasing customer retention—keeping current customers actively involved in doing business because their needs are met and they are never tempted to look elsewhere for better service.

Customer service is an important part of the overall marketing strategy; this has encouraged the development of some nontraditional approaches. One example of a nontraditional approach to customer service is offering informational newsletters to customers. Informational newsletters sent periodically (by e-mail or traditional mail) or handed out are nonthreatening to customers because they share information, new product or service offerings, new systems, or service hours; they also remind customers that the company is available and ready to serve them again. Newsletters have the luxury of being seen by customers as informational pieces that are not trying to sell something. They are really selling the company, but the approach is subtler; therefore, it is less threatening.

KEY TERMS

credibility	perception	scope of influence
ethics	primary expectations	secondary expectations
expectations	reputation management	values

QUICK QUIZ

1. Laziness, poor communications skills, moodiness, inability to handle stress, and inadequate staff are all enhancements to customer service.   T or F
2. The way we see something based on our experience is our perception.   T or F
3. Expectations are always negative. T or F
4. Expectations are always based on our perceptions.   T or F
5. The average scope of influence that an individual has is between seven and fifteen people.   T or F
6. The reputation of a company really is not important to prospective customers.   T or F
7. Our personal credibility can be the one characteristic that determines our success as people and as customer service providers.   T or F
8. Once credibility is lost, it is easy to regain. T or F
9. Ethics are a set of principles that govern the conduct of an individual or group.   T or F
10. It is always popular to do the right thing and to have high ethical standards.   T or F

OPPORTUNITIES FOR CRITICAL THINKING

1. Why is it important to convey credibility to your customer?
2. Explain the five techniques for exceeding customers' expectations.
3. Why do many people talk about customer service and yet do little to improve its quality?
4. Why should we consider our customers' perceptions?
5. What are some common barriers to customer service?
6. How relevant is the reality that some customers may perceive your service inaccurately?
7. How do primary expectations differ from secondary expectations?
8. Describe an example of a situation where scope of influence hurt or helped your business.
9. What are some techniques for conveying credibility to others?
10. What role do values play in an individual's approach to providing customer service?

SKILL BUILDING

Understanding Expectations

All customers have their own unique sets of expectations. Expectations may be positive or negative. Organizations must periodically attempt to determine what their customers expect from their customer experience.

Individually or in small groups of three or four, list the top four expectations that customers would have of the following organizations:

- Prestige hotel
- Electric company
- Nationally recognized fast-food chain
- Auto service department or garage
- Car rental company
- Local community college
- Credit card company
- Your own organization or department

After determining the top four expectations of each of the preceding organizations, rank the expectations from easiest to provide to most difficult. Attempt to draw conclusions from your rankings.

A common observation when customer expectations are evaluated is that many of the expectations that customers have are easy and inexpensive to provide. Attempting to understand customers' expectations gives organizations the opportunity to consistently strive to be what customers want them to be.

Ethics in Action

The local news has been reporting that your company is going to be announcing a big layoff. In case you are one of the unlucky ones that is laid off should you create and print your resume at work? What if everyone else is doing it?

CHALLENGE   # Personal Purpose Statement

The concept that each of us has a purpose is not a new one, but it is one that we are hearing a lot about today. Although there are numerous ways of interpreting our individual "purpose," in this activity we concentrate on your individual, personal purpose. As each of us goes through our daily lives and routines, it is helpful to focus on our purpose or the *reason we exist*. This is a question that can have a variety of answers that will likely change at different times in our lives. The defining of our personal purpose can help to keep us focused on goals, sustain us during difficult times, reward us with a sense of accomplishment, and remind us to always strive to be the best that we can be.

Challenge Objectives

1. To demonstrate an understanding of how to define an individual's personal purpose
2. To identify the combination of unique individual characteristics, talents, goals, and requirements that work together to define "why we exist"
3. To present in written form an individualized, personal purpose statement

Assignment

As you work toward determining your personal purpose statement, you may want to ask yourself some of the following questions:

- What do I enjoy doing?
- When am I the happiest?

- What could I do better?
- What do I believe is important?
- What do I see myself doing in five years?
- What am I good at?
- What is my proudest accomplishment?
- Do I enjoy being/working with others or prefer to be/work alone?
- How do I want others to think of me?
- How do I want others to remember me?

You may want to create additional questions that are appropriate for you. Asking yourself these questions will give you a lot of information to work with, but it will also allow you to detect a pattern of priorities that you might not have recognized before.

Presentation

Present in written form your personal purpose statement. Your statement should be professionally written in a concise manner. Individual paragraphs may address different areas of your life; or one complete paragraph is acceptable. Submit to your instructor *two* copies of your purpose statement. One copy is for grading purposes to be returned to you; the second copy should be submitted in a self-addressed, stamped envelope. Your instructor will mail this envelope to you later in your class term. It is easy to be motivated as you are establishing goals and defining your purpose, but as time goes by it is easy to get caught up in your busy life and to forget "why" you exist. Your personal purpose statement will arrive via mail, and you can be reminded as to "why you exist."

ANSWERS TO QUICK QUIZ

1. F	5. T	9. T
2. T	6. F	10. F
3. F	7. T	
4. F	8. F	

Problem Solving

Remember This

We are continually faced by great opportunities brilliantly disguised as insoluble problems.

CHAPTER OBJECTIVES

In this chapter, you will learn how to

- Define problem solving.
- Explain the problem-solving process.
- Describe the use of brainstorming and diagramming as problem-solving strategies.

- Illustrate mind mapping.
- Develop negotiation skills.
- Use follow-up to problem solving as a customer service tool.

◀ Role of Problem Solving in Customer Service

Most individuals encounter the need to solve problems frequently. In many instances, problems are challenges that we would prefer to avoid; but, in most cases, this is not a possibility. One of the most important activities in which most customer service providers participate is helping to solve customers' problems. **Problem solving** is an active resolution to a challenging situation.

Many individuals dread problem solving. It can add considerable stress to an otherwise peaceful work environment. One of the main reasons problem solving is perceived as being unpleasant is because the average business professional has not worked to develop the skills necessary to accomplish it effectively and efficiently. The only training that some people have is their observations of their own families dealing with problems as they were growing up. This example is frequently not transferable to a business environment. Most individuals in an organization are aware of the repercussions that can result from an incorrect resolution to problems. Because of this, they may be reluctant to take the responsibility that accompanies problem solving.

To actively confront the challenge of problem solving, organizations must prepare employees with training. They must create a safe environment that encourages employees to develop solutions that are positive for both the customer and the company.

Problem solving and decision making are individualized processes. Every individual may have his or her own method of determining an appropriate course of action. What is important is the end result, not the process of determining the solution. As long as the solution is timely, the process is less important.

One significant challenge to problem solving when interacting with customers is the speed with which decisions must be made. When a customer calls with a question or problem, the customer service provider may only have a few seconds or minutes to provide an answer. Unfortunately, this does not allow for much time to examine possible solutions. Customer service providers must become highly proficient in listening to a customer's explanation of a situation or problem, in asking pertinent questions to clarify the information, and in providing the customer with an appropriate solution. The solution must be one that they are willing to share regardless of the possible repercussions.

Customer service providers can effectively equip themselves to make decisions and to solve problems by learning problem-solving strategies, developing negotiation skills, learning how to deal effectively with conflict, and recognizing the importance of follow-up.

◀ **problem solving**
An active resolution to a challenging situation.

Creativity and Problem Solving

When individuals incorporate creativity into the process of problem solving, positive challenges result. Creative problem solving suggests that through an open approach to finding solutions, an appropriate and innovative result may be discovered. Creative problem solving requires that employees work in a culture that allows new ideas to flow freely and to be considered realistically. When the same problems consistently arise and are resolved in the same established manner, the opportunity for new and more creative resolutions may exist.

Customers appreciate creativity. Creativity requires effort and commitment to creating a new idea or solution. The individuals in an organization who are the closest to the pulse of the customers are those individuals who interact with them on an ongoing basis. In many organizations, these individuals are the customer service providers. By offering suggestions to customers and to management about innovative ways of solving challenges, customer service providers can share their creativity with others.

Problems as Opportunities

Criticism provides an opportunity to obtain information. When customers express problems or frustrations, it is easy to become defensive. A productive method of response to criticism is to consider the criticism as productive input to the creation of a problem-solving environment. A customer complaint is really a request for action.

Customers frequently have ideas about how a problem may be avoided in the future. Offering them the opportunity to share their ideas gives customers the opportunity to participate in the process of improving a situation or system that has disappointed them. This allows a team effort that creates unity between provider and customer.

Confronting Conflict

Conflict is a reality of most approaches to problem solving. Problem solving and decision making involve the consideration of possible alternatives and the selection of the alternative that is viewed by the decision maker as the most appropriate. This does not mean that all of the parties involved will agree that the chosen course of action is the best. This may create conflict in some situations. **Conflict** is a hostile encounter that occurs as a result of opposing needs, wishes, or ideas. Conflict can occur in even the most

conflict A hostile encounter that occurs as a result of opposing needs, wishes, or ideas.

cohesive employee team or with our most faithful customers. When faced with conflict and disagreement, it is important to proceed with caution! Many words have been spoken in anger, creating difficult-to-correct damage. The goal in any problem-solving environment, even when anger is present, is not to win an argument but to resolve a conflict.

When encountering conflict, remember the following suggestions:

1. Listen to the other viewpoints that are being presented.
2. Do not bring up old problems from the past or assign blame.
3. Use tact as you respond to others.
4. Do not repress your own anger; instead, use it productively. Take advantage of the opportunity to share other related concerns in a positive manner.
5. Focus on finding the best solution to the conflict.

"A professional is someone who can do his best work when he doesn't feel like it."
Alistair Cooke

Problem-Solving Process

Numerous approaches may be taken when attempting to solve problems. After determining that a problem exists, it is helpful to respond to the following guidelines. The guidelines are represented as they occur in the problem-solving model shown in Figure 1.

1. **Identify the problem:** Attempt to recognize and understand what the real problem is. Sometimes the true problem will be difficult to identify because of other variables that are more recognizable but that do not represent the problem that requires solving.
2. **Understand the problem's unique characteristics and the possible outcomes:** The problems that must be solved by customer service providers are frequently confounded by unique characteristics. These unique characteristics may have no bearing on the eventual solution, but they must be considered while a solution is being developed.
3. **Define the requirements of a possible solution considering the company policies currently in place:** Frequent requests may have resulted in policies being developed to promote consistency in solutions. The requirements of the solution must be determined and the policies considered. Policies that are flexible should be considered as opportunities.
4. **Identify possible solutions:** Frequently, the success of a problem's solution has to do with the generation of more than one possible solution and the selection of the best solution. As possible solutions are considered, they should reflect an array of alternatives and the individuals who will be affected.
5. **Select the best solution:** Selecting the best solution may be the most challenging aspect of the problem-solving process. The positive and negative results must be considered from both the company's and the customer's perspective.

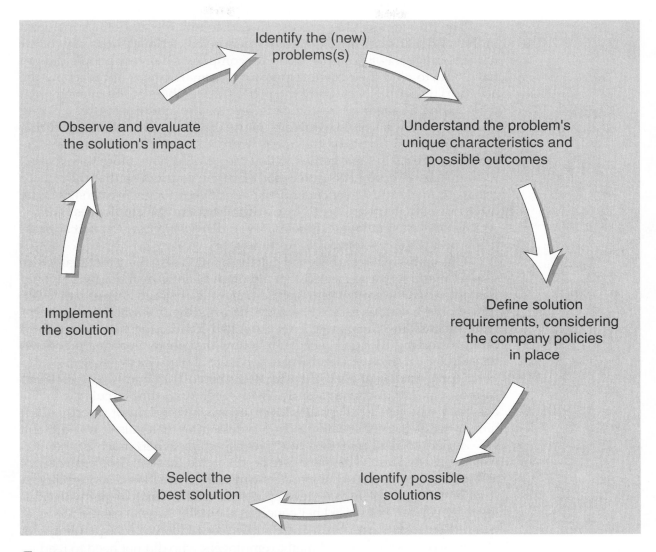

Identify the (new) problems(s)

Understand the problem's unique characteristics and possible outcomes

Observe and evaluate the solution's impact

Define solution requirements, considering the company policies in place

Implement the solution

Select the best solution

Identify possible solutions

FIGURE 1   The Problem-Solving Model

6. **Implement the solution, informing the customer of the details and how the customer will be affected:** Putting the solution into place is an integral part of the problem-solving process. From the customer's viewpoint, nothing has been done until the solution is implemented. The most creative solution has little value if it is not put into action. Communication is important at this time. Everyone who will be affected by the solution must be informed of its implementation and of any responsibility that they may have in contributing to its success.

7. **Observe and evaluate the solution's impact:** After a solution has been implemented, it should be observed and evaluated to determine whether it was successful. Observation can occur on an ongoing basis, but a formal evaluation should be scheduled to take place at a designated time.

The problem-solving process should follow the guidelines included in the model. If steps are skipped or overlooked, serious errors may occur in the solutions. For example, a courier company's delivery people did not have time to read their mail. Important information was not reaching the appropriate people because of the problem. Members of the management team called a meeting to attempt to resolve the situation. After hearing a brief explanation of the problem, members of the group began sharing their solutions. Some of the ideas were to begin forwarding all the employees' mail to their homes so that they would have more time to read it, to purchase laptop computers for all of the couriers so that they could receive e-mail, and to reprimand the employees for their oversight. The most popular solution was to forward the mail to the employees' homes. At this time, the management team began discussing how to print address labels and what type of envelopes to use.

One of the managers believed that the solution of mailing materials twice was premature. She suggested that although mailing material twice would guarantee that the employees received their mail, it would not guarantee that they would actually read it. She suggested finding out *why* the employees were not reading their mail. This provoked a more focused approach to problem solving. The group began to follow the problem-solving process as they attempted to understand and to solve the mail problem.

Upon further analysis, it was determined that employees received as many as 100 documents daily. Every memorandum circulated in the company was sent to every employee, even when it did not directly affect him or her. A courier's main function is delivering materials; it was difficult for couriers to read mail and to drive, especially when much of the mail was useless to them. The managers began to see that the problem was not just with the employees; the management team shared the responsibility. A solution to the problem was developed to meet the needs of all involved. If the manager had not voiced her concerns about the original solution to what was perceived as the problem, the company would have been spending a lot of money on postage to send mail to employees who did not need to read it.

TEAM TIME

Sit down with your team and identify a recurring problem within your department/group. Referring to the *problem-solving model*, specifically identify the problem and follow the steps for problem solving detailed in the model. Be sure to encourage and accept all group members' input. Be as creative as company policies and circumstances will allow. Establish a time line to review the solution to evaluate how well it is working. Upon evaluation, celebrate your success or make modifications for future success. The more you use the problem-solving model, the easier it will be to determine the positive results!

Problem-Solving Strategies

When approaching the challenge of determining a solution for a problem, individual strategies or a combination of strategies may be used. To effectively determine solutions, it may be helpful to follow methods that have been proven to create positive results. The two common strategies of problem solving are brainstorming and diagramming.

Brainstorming

Brainstorming is a problem-solving strategy that can be used by groups of two or more. The premise behind brainstorming is that the more ideas that are shared in an open and accepting environment, the more creativity will result. As ideas are shared, other ideas may develop. A group approach like brainstorming to problem solving can create a unique and creative opportunity to generate solutions.

To begin a brainstorming exercise, a group gathers willing to share ideas. A specific problem is identified. One individual is designated as the recorder; he or she is responsible for recording the ideas shared.

The next step is for someone to share the first idea. Other ideas should follow. The more ideas shared, the better, as ideas frequently stimulate other ideas. It is mandatory for the leaders facilitating the exercise to create an accepting environment in which the participants can operate. If individuals are afraid that their ideas will be rejected or that they will be ridiculed for their suggestions, they will be less likely to participate.

When several ideas have been generated, a master list is prepared. It can be displayed immediately on a flipchart or whiteboard. The master list can also be compiled and distributed to group members for later discussion. The members can review the ideas and make additions. A second meeting should be held to recommend the most appropriate solutions. Allowing group members to review all the ideas that were shared makes it easier to determine which ideas are possible solutions to the problem. Implementation of the chosen solutions can begin, and the problem is on its way to being resolved.

Diagramming

Diagramming is a strategy for problem solving that provides a visual representation of the problem and the facts related to it. Visual representations are easy to work with because they allow visual examination as well as discussion. There are four main methods of diagramming problems in search of appropriate solutions: pro/con sheets, flowcharts, organizational charts, and mind mapping.

1. Pro/con sheets: A simple approach to diagramming a problem is the use of pro/con sheets (Figure 2). Pro/con sheets are best when used to choose a specific course of action as the resolution to a problem. To create a pro/con sheet, write the problem and the possible solution on a sheet of

◄ brainstorming
A problem-solving strategy that can be used by groups of two or more.

◄ diagramming
A strategy for problem solving that provides a visual representation of the problem and the facts related to it.

◄ pro/con sheets
A simple approach to diagramming a problem that involves recording the arguments for and against a solution.

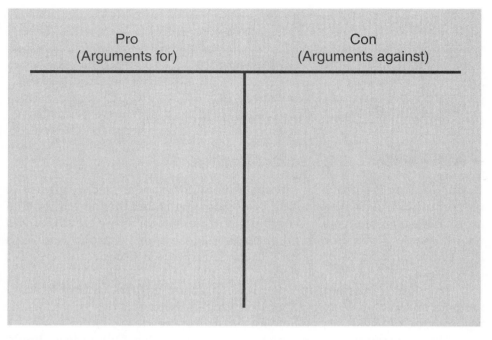

| Pro
(Arguments for) | Con
(Arguments against) |

FIGURE 2 Pro/Con Sheet

paper. Then draw a line down the center and write the word *pro* on one side and *con* on the other side. Write all the positive reasons that the solution would work on the *pro* side of the line. List all the reasons why the solution would not be appropriate on the *con* side. When all the reasons for and against a possible solution are listed, it can be determined whether the solution is appropriate or not. Pro/con sheets are simple, which is one reason that they can work well in choosing a solution.

flowcharts
A diagramming approach to problem solving that charts each step of a process to assist in determining why a problem is occurring.

2. Flowcharts: When using flowcharts in the problem-solving process, it is helpful to diagram what the process or flow of a problem is (Figure 3). Sometimes just listing how a situation is processed and who must be involved is enough to identify why a problem is occurring. To create a flowchart, include in a box on the top of a sheet of paper the point where a process begins. An example may be: Who has to authorize an extension on a payment for a customer? If the beginning of the process starts with the customer making the request, this goes in the first box. The person whom the customer calls goes in the second box. The third box is for the person whom the employee must ask to gain approval for the payment extension. If the customer's records must be retrieved from another department, this goes in the next box. The process continues from there.

Diagramming the current system for responding to the customer's request makes it easier to understand why the process takes longer than may be considered appropriate. Flowcharts are helpful in identifying unnecessary steps in a process. They can also assist in identifying who would be affected by a change in the method of processing information.

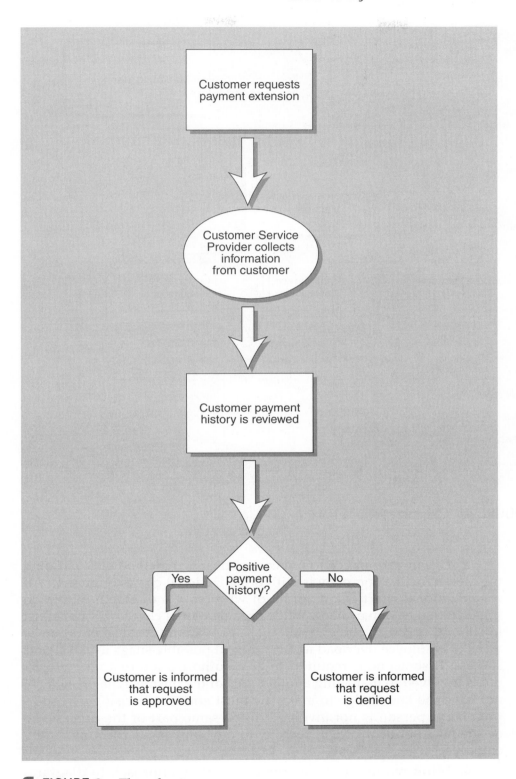

FIGURE 3 Flowchart

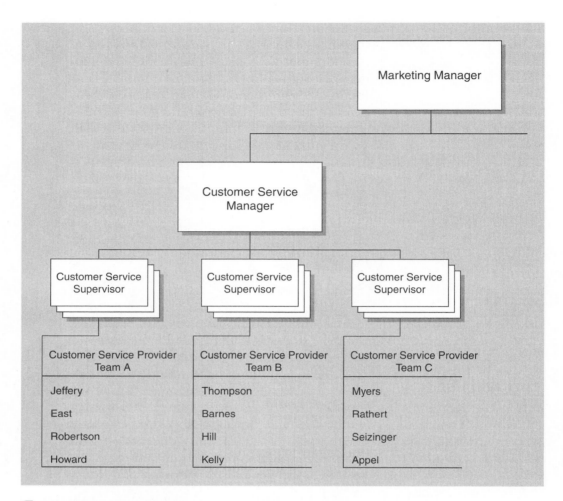

◀ **FIGURE 4**   Organizational Chart

◀ **organizational charts**   A method of illustrating the hierarchy of a company by illustrating who reports to whom.

◀ **mind mapping** A creative approach to diagramming a problem in which a problem is recorded on paper and possible solutions branch out from the original problem.

3. Organizational charts: A commonly used method of illustrating the hierarchy of a company is with organizational charts (Figure 4). An organizational chart is a diagram of who reports to whom within an organization or department. While organizational charts will not assist in solving specific problems, they can provide a visual illustration of areas of employee overload and can reveal possible snags in a system's success. If someone is required to give authorization to a new project but is involved in managing another area of the business, he or she may not have the knowledge to make the most effective decisions. In addition, if the person is not involved in the same part of the process, he or she may not be aware of the day-to-day challenges encountered by employees.

4. Mind mapping: An extremely creative approach to diagramming a problem is mind mapping (Figure 5). The concept of mind map-

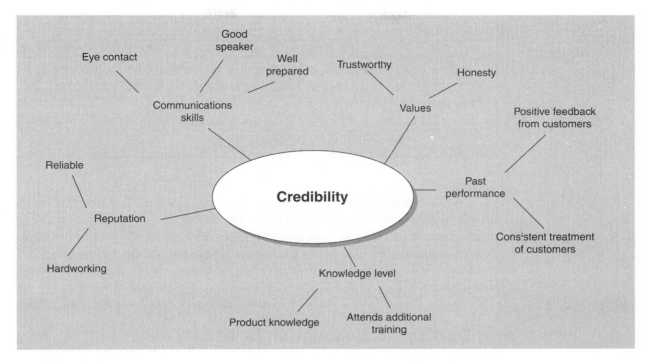

FIGURE 5 Mind Mapping

ping was developed in the 1970s and is still popular today. Mind mapping involves the practical aspects of traditional problem solving while incorporating the opportunity to freely approach new ways of thinking.

To begin a mind map, place the problem or decision in an oval in the center of a large piece of paper. The center placement symbolizes that the problem or decision is the core of your map. After creating the center, place lines going out of the center in different directions. On the lines, write important words or phrases that pertain to finding a solution to the challenge. Add additional branches coming off the important words or phrases. These branches should list ideas or thoughts that relate to the solution of the problem. Try to come up with ideas as quickly as possible; the more outlandish and creative the ideas are, the better. Quality is not important at this point in the process. If visual images can illustrate ideas, it is appropriate to use them. Record as many ideas as possible. Review the ideas and make additions if any are suggested. Try putting aside your mind map for an hour or even a day, and then review what you have written. Make any additions that you can. Then begin drawing conclusions from your "map." What solutions have been diagrammed that could possibly be implemented? Share your ideas with others and seek their feedback.

Job Link

Create a pro/con sheet for a decision that you need to make. It can be as simple as where to go for lunch or as complex as whether or not you should make a job change. Make your list as quickly as you can and then review the results. Sometimes a pro/con sheet is the most effective (and easiest) way to work toward a decision. Give it a try!

When mind mapping, it is important to approach the exercise with an open mind and a willingness to think creatively. Mind mapping is not meant to be neat and orderly or even consistently realistic. It is meant to stimulate ideas and to help individuals consider what may be possible. Many people write speeches and plan meetings by creating mind maps.

Developing Negotiation Skills

There may be no easy solutions to problems in a professional environment. Customer complaints, requests, and problems must be resolved in an efficient manner. A constructive method of problem solving is to ask the customer what will resolve the situation. While this places responsibility on the customer to share what he or she sees as a satisfactory resolution, it also places a significant responsibility on the individual whose job it is to decide what an appropriate resolution would be. At this time, the art of successful negotiation is necessary.

negotiation
The evaluation of the possible solutions to a challenge and the selection of the solution that is mutually beneficial.

Negotiation is the evaluation of the possible solutions to a challenge and the selection of the solution that is mutually beneficial. Negotiation requires discussion between the two parties involved. It suggests that a resolution can be reached that everyone involved considers fair and reasonable. Negotiation must allow for give and take on both sides of an issue. To improve negotiation skills as a customer service provider, remember the following suggestions:

1. Know your customer: Anyone involved in solving a problem must know the parties involved. Past relationships can shed valuable light on how a customer may approach a current situation. New customers have unique qualities that we have yet to discover. The more familiar we can become with our customers, the more likely we will be to recognize what their real problems or concerns are. Some customers may make outrageous requests initially and then lessen their demands. If this tendency has been noticed previously, it is helpful to recall it at the beginning of the negotiation process.

Customers are unique individuals with their own sets of needs, motivations, and fears. The greater our awareness of their needs, motivations, and fears, the more effectively we can begin to solve their problems. Customers want to know that they are important to us and to our business. They also want to know that we remember them from one interaction to another. Any details that we can draw on about specific customers can help us to solve their problems appropriately.

2. Ask questions and listen to the spoken and unspoken messages: By asking questions of our customers and actively listening to their responses, we can develop an informed understanding of the situation at hand. The more information that can be collected, the more accurately we can help to solve the customers' problems. Customers are not always eager to share all the details of a situation. Effective questioning requires that the customer service provider continue to ask questions until he or she believes that all of the pertinent information has been collected. Once questions have been answered, it is helpful for customer service providers to clarify their understanding by reviewing their interpretation of what the customer has shared.

Customers may have unspoken messages that they are unwilling to share with others without some type of encouragement. Customers who are unable to pay their bills because of sudden changes in their lives may not feel comfortable sharing their problems with someone else. In this situation, the customer service provider must "listen" to what the customer is not saying. This can be done by listening to the hesitation that a customer may have in responding to a question, by attempting to detect anxiety in their voice, or by asking nonthreatening questions that convey to the customer that meeting their current needs is of utmost importance. Although customers who are having cash flow problems may be reluctant to share the details of their situations, they will be pleased to learn about a company's special payment opportunities or other possible alternatives.

Sometimes asking a customer questions creates tension in a conversation. Customers may not want to share more information than they think is necessary. By asking well-presented questions, the customer service provider can create an environment in which the customer may be more willing to share the details that can lead to problem resolution. Questions must be asked with a tone of empathy. Customers need to know that they are important and that their best interest is the company's concern.

3. Know the policies of your organization and in which areas flexibility is allowed: When attempting to negotiate with customers, it is especially important to be very familiar with your company's policies. It is hard to coordinate a resolution to a situation if you are uninformed about what will be allowed. Not knowing company policies may make customer service providers appear unprepared or as though they have little or no authority. No customer wants to hear that the reason that his or her requests cannot be granted is because it is against "company policy," but in many cases this is the only response that is accurate. Knowing what is not allowed is not enough. Customer service providers can go into a negotiation situation ready to negotiate if they also know what the policies allow. Unfortunately, all too often human beings focus on what cannot be done rather than what can be done.

Most policies have been developed to establish a consistent method of responding to a common situation. In this respect, policies are a positive measure that a company has taken so that it is not accused of showing favoritism among its customers. Customers may not always think of the existence of policies in this way. Customer service providers should know where and when flexibility is allowed with regard to policies. If customer service providers are trained and empowered, they will comprehend the amount of flexibility that they can exercise on behalf of their customers.

4. Demonstrate the willingness to be flexible: The ability to react to situations as they occur is important in demonstrating flexibility. It is not enough to want to grant the customer's request; customer service providers must be able to convey that desire to their customers. By asking customers how they would suggest that a situation be resolved, an opening for their input has been suggested. If their suggestions can be entirely or even partially implemented, the customers may feel as though they have created a positive solution that the company was flexible enough to agree to. Flexibility can also be expressed through the words used in interacting with customers. Encouraging words that express appreciation for the customers' ideas are always a plus. Whenever possible, allow customers to participate in the problem-solving and negotiation process. Their ideas may be inspired because of their involvement in the overall situation. Their approach to the problem resolution may even be more conservative than the one that the company might have offered.

5. Learn to handle your anger and your customer's anger appropriately: In a situation in which negotiation is taking place, anger is always a possibility. Something has taken the situation to the point of requiring negotiation. When anger is revealed, it is best to defuse it as subtly as possible. Anger may express frustration, anxiety, or unmet expectations. It may also be a result of circumstances totally unrelated to the situation being discussed.

To defuse a customer's anger, try to anticipate the cause and to confront it carefully. Anger that is defused quickly is less likely to build in intensity. The customer service provider can acknowledge that a change in the situation could occur and could offer some type of compensation. A customer who is annoyed because he or she has been waiting in line at a drive-up window at a fast-food restaurant may angrily ask the manager what the holdup is. The manager may respond by saying that several employees called in sick and that they are understaffed. This response alone may make the customer even angrier, but when the manager offers free food or drinks to compensate for the customer's inconvenience, the anger may begin to diminish. By offering the apology and the free items, the manager is acknowledging that his company is in error, but he is minimizing the effect of the error.

Whenever possible, shift responsibility for the customer's anger back to the customer. This must be done with care, but it can have positive results. A customer may call his or her lawn care company, ready to cancel the contract because of recurring weeds. When the company owner hears that the customer is concerned about the weed problem, he or she can respond immediately by saying that if the customer will call in the future, the company will provide an additional application at no cost. Although the owner does not say it, he is reminding the customer that it would be impossible for the lawn care company to recheck all of the customers' lawns to determine the effectiveness of each application. By encouraging the customer to share in the responsibility, anger may be defused and the business relationship may continue. This approach would not be effective if frequently repeated; however, if used periodically, it could be effective.

When customer service providers find that they are becoming angry, they should consider the role that they are playing as representatives of their company. Every individual must take responsibility for his or her own anger. A company's reputation will not be enhanced if the employees allow their anger to be shown to customers. When you feel yourself becoming angry, move quickly to resolve the challenging situation.

6. Consider what the customer may lose in the negotiation process: The nature of negotiation involves give and take. Customers may feel that they are doing all of the giving and that the company is doing all of the taking. Try to understand what the customer will see as a compromise. A customer who is delinquent in bill payment may be seeking to be relieved of some of the financial responsibility. Although this may be an unrealistic solution from the company's viewpoint, the customer may not see it that way. A modified payment schedule may be the solution to the situation, but the customer still must pay. When negotiating with customers, stress that the goal is a positive resolution for all.

7. Determine mutually beneficial solutions to challenging problems and situations: When completing a negotiation with a customer, seek solutions that will benefit both the company and the customer. No one gains if the customer leaves the interaction angry, vowing never to do business with the company again. By creating a win–win situation that both sides can live with, potential future business relationships can be a possibility. Even if it has been determined that a company no longer wishes to do business with a customer, it must be remembered that possible business contacts with others who are acquainted with the difficult customer are probably desired.

Explain to the customer exactly how the agreed-upon solution will work. Seek feedback from the customer so that additional information can be provided if necessary. Stress that the solution allowed both sides to compromise, but the result will have a positive benefit for all.

Professional Approaches to Apologizing and Conveying Bad News

As customer service providers attempt to assist their customers in problem solving, they may become aware of errors or oversights that were made by their own company, by coworkers, or by themselves. Effective problem solving acknowledges the fact that the customers may have legitimate concerns and that the customer was treated inappropriately. At this time, an apology is due to the customer. Apologies are not signs of weakness, but instead they are productive methods of continuing the opportunity to communicate.

Apologizing to customers is a reality of professional life. While customer service providers should not apologize without justification, they should be prepared to do so when appropriate.

When apologizing to customers, consider the following suggestions:

1. **Acknowledge customers' feelings:** By indicating to customers that we recognize their feelings and emotions, we send the message that we care.
2. **Express to the customer that you share the responsibility for the problem:** Even if you and your company were only loosely associated with the problem, you are a part of its diagnosis and resolution.
3. **Convey sincerity:** When apologizing to customers, it is important to convey care and concern. If we say that we regret that an error was made, the manner in which we say it should demonstrate our regret.
4. **Ask for the opportunity to correct the problem:** Just apologizing for a problem has little impact if we do not offer to correct the error or to make changes in the future. Saying "May we correct the error for you?" expresses the desire to continue doing business with the customer.
5. **Request the opportunity to continue doing business in the future:** By asking the customer if we can still consider him or her an active customer, we suggest to the customer that we are willing to correct the error and would like to go forward in a positive business relationship. This request also gives the customer the opportunity to share other concerns that might keep him or her from doing business with us.

> *Success is how high you bounce when you hit bottom.*
> **General George Patton**

Barriers to Problem Solving and Decision Making

A number of barriers may exist that affect the actuality of problem solving and decision making. Decision makers may not be aware that barriers are detracting from the decision-making process. Some of the most common barriers to problem solving and decision making are as follows:

- **Resistance to change:** People are often reluctant to change from the time-honored way of doing things. Resistance to change can prevent people from taking chances and from considering new possibilities.
- **Habits:** Habits limit our vision of what can be accomplished and may stand in the way of solving a problem. Habits may go undetected

by an individual and may be a tremendous deterrent to correcting a problem. For example, a receptionist who is having difficulty completing his or her work may be unaware that the habit of taking personal calls is taking the bulk of his or her work time.

- **Individual insecurity:** Individual insecurity may deter individuals from taking risks or from pursuing behavior that may require them to take a stand. Individual insecurity may come from past experiences or from an overall lack of self-confidence.
- **Past history:** Knowing what has happened before and what worked and did not work can inhibit an individual's desire to try new methods of problem solving or decision making. Past history is frequently an excuse for not making changes. The individual who may not wish to approach a situation in a new way may remind others that a similar idea failed in the past.
- **Fear of success or failure:** At some time, everyone experiences some type of fear. The fear of success or failure may be viewed as unreasonable, but it can greatly deter the confrontation of problems. The unknown can be a frightening thing. When a new way of doing something is attempted, the possibility exists that it may work well or not at all. In either instance, changes may result. While some people thrive on recognition, others shy away from it. These fears may cause people to avoid the possibility of success or failure altogether.
- **Jumping to conclusions:** When problems must be solved and decisions made, it is easy to jump to conclusions. When someone jumps to conclusions, assumptions are made about what may or may not work or the possible results; assumptions may frequently take on negative perspectives.
- **Perceptions:** As we have stated, perceptions are the ways that we see things based on our experiences. We may be unable to see something from another perspective because we are so blinded by our own perception.

By developing an awareness of some of the barriers to problem solving and decision making, customer service providers can attempt to overcome the obstacles before they occur.

Importance of Follow-Up in Problem Solving

Once a problem or problems have been solved or decisions have been made, it is vitally important to follow up. **Follow-up** is checking back to determine whether or not a situation is operating according to the initial plan. Effective follow-up requires that the original problem solver or decision maker check back with the customer to determine whether or not the original plan of action actually took place. The most effective approach to problem solving has little value if the solution was never fully implemented or if it has run into some type of difficulty. Customers remember the end of their interaction, not the beginning or the middle. A customer may have

follow-up
Checking back to determine whether or not a situation is operating according to the initial plan.

been treated in a friendly manner, had questions answered quickly, and been highly satisfied with a solution that was created to correct his or her problem; however, if for some reason the solution never took place, the customer will not remember the friendly treatment. The customer will remember that he or she still has a problem that needs to be resolved. Anytime a solution to a problem requires the involvement of someone other than the person making the commitment, follow-up should occur.

Keeping customers informed about the status of their order or problem even when there is no news to report can be an excellent public relations tool. A periodic call just to let customers know that you have not forgotten them or their concern can be a refreshing change from the treatment that the customers may be accustomed to receiving. Their response may be, "I cannot believe that you called me back! Your company really does provide excellent customer service." Follow-up is a safeguard to ensure that customers continue to be satisfied with a company and its ability to meet the needs of its customers.

Through effective preparation, the reality of problem solving and decision making in customer service can become an active opportunity to convey to customers how valuable they are to the success of a business and that satisfying their needs is a part of the accomplishment of a company's goals.

KEY TERMS

brainstorming

conflict

diagramming

flowcharts

follow-up

mind mapping

negotiation

organizational charts

problem solving

pro/con sheets

QUICK QUIZ

1. Problem solving is an active resolution to a challenging situation.   T or F
2. Customers overwhelmingly oppose the use of creativity in problem solving.   T or F
3. Speed is not an important factor to customers when they have a problem to be solved.   T or F
4. Conflict is a hostile encounter that occurs as a result of opposing needs, wishes, or ideas.   T or F
5. Brainstorming is an effective problem-solving strategy for individuals to use. T or F
6. Flowcharts are a simple approach to diagramming a problem that involves recording the arguments for and against a solution.   T or F
7. Showing anger to a customer is appropriate. T or F
8. The solutions that customer service providers come up with are always right.   T or F
9. Habits can be a barrier to problem solving. T or F
10. Follow-up is not important. Customers remember the beginning of an interaction, not the end.   T or F

OPPORTUNITIES FOR CRITICAL THINKING

1. Explain the problem-solving model and the seven steps to determining and implementing a solution.
2. How can brainstorming provide the opportunity for creative problem solving?
3. Why is it helpful for organizations to train their employees in possible approaches to problem solving?
4. How can the use of creativity in problem solving more effectively address unique situations?
5. A positive way to view problems is to think of them as opportunities. How can this approach reduce the temptation to respond defensively to customers' problems or frustrations?
6. Discuss some guidelines to follow when encountering conflict.
7. Why is a simple approach to problem solving, like the use of pro/con sheets, frequently the most productive?
8. Select a problem or decision to be made and create a mind map to explore possible solutions.
9. Why is an understanding of your company's policies important when negotiating a solution to a challenge?
10. How important is follow-up to the solution of a problem?

SKILL BUILDING

Problem Solving and Decision Making

Most customer service interactions require that problems be rectified and that decisions be made. Customer service providers have to equip themselves to analyze situations and to efficiently determine appropriate solutions.

Using the problem-solving strategies, determine your own solutions to the following "What would you do?" scenarios:

- The accounts receivable department that you manage has been having problems with customers not paying their bills on time. An additional problem is that numerous customers are sending the wrong portion of their bill with their payment. It has been suggested that the real problem is that the billing statement needs a new, more readable look.

  Applying one of the problem-solving strategies, determine the most appropriate solution to this problem.

- You have recently been feeling dissatisfied in your position as a reservation associate at a nationally recognized car rental company. There are opportunities for advancement at your current company, but you might like to look elsewhere for a new opportunity.

  Applying one or more of the problem-solving strategies, determine an appropriate direction to take.

- In your position of corporate trainer, you have noticed that many of your trainees/customers are not following through with the assignments that you give them and that frequently they are not prepared for presentations when they are due.

  Consider the problem-solving strategies and use at least one to determine a solution to this situation.

Ethics in Action

You are the manager of a local "box type" store. Customers come to you to stock up on basic items and to get great prices on everyday products. Today a couple came to one of your checkout stands. They wanted to know how they could get the gift card that was promised following a $50.00 purchase of some specific items. The checker did not know anything about this promotion. She called her supervisor and the supervisor indicated to the customer that your company never did that type of promotion and that the customers were wrong. The customers became visibly upset and said that they had traveled from another community to make the purchase and receive the gift card. The supervisor also told them to go home and reread the ad and if they were correct bring it into the store. At this point, the customers passed on their desired purchase and checked out their other items. They immediately asked to speak to you. Now you must solve the problem. How do you keep these customers satisfied and willing to continue to do business with you in the future? Incidentally, you don't know anything about the ad in the newspaper either but it really DID run.

CHALLENGE

Research Activity

Today, more than any other time in history, people are seeking information. It has become easy to research almost anything on which an individual or group may need information. The ability to collect and compile accurate research is a skill that all professionals need to develop. While it is fun and easy to get information, the ability to sift through information and to compile it into usable form is an important part of formulating informed conclusions.

Challenge Objectives

1. To provide individuals with the opportunity for additional research in an area of customer service of their choice.
2. To compile information collected in a concise and factual written report.
3. For individuals to orally share information in their report with others.

Assignment

With your instructor, choose a topic relevant in customer service to research. Try to find a topic that not only will have available information but also is of interest to you. If it can help you in your current or future employment, even better! Conduct your research in an organized and professional manner. The Internet is a wonderful research tool that is used commonly by today's professionals, but try to confirm the validity of the information you collect. Just because information is found on the Internet (or anywhere else), it is not necessarily true.

Research your chosen topic as extensively as possible. Attempt to acquire a well-rounded perspective on your topic.

You should have a minimum of four sources of information. One of your sources should be from the Internet. You may use several sources from the Internet, but at least one source should come from another place. A personal interview with a professional is an interesting way to supplement your other information and can provide a real-world perspective.

Presentation   Compile the information that you have gathered into a written report. Reports should be well written and easily understood. All reports are to be typed and should be five to eight pages in length. Footnotes are not necessary, but endnotes should be included to accurately credit your sources.

Reports should be presented informally to the class by each individual. This will allow all participants to benefit from your research.

Have fun with your research. The topic that you choose will probably be one that you will be interested in for years to come!

ANSWERS TO QUICK QUIZ

1.	T	5.	T	9.	T
2.	F	6.	F	10.	F
3.	F	7.	F		
4.	T	8.	F		

Strategy for Formulating a Plan for Success

From Chapter 4 of *Customer Service: A Practical Approach.* Sixth Edition. Elaine K. Harris. Copyright © 2013 by Pearson Education, Inc. All rights reserved.

Strategy for Formulating a Plan for Success

Remember This

Quality is never an accident; it is always the result of high intention, sincere effort, intelligent direction, and skillful execution; it represents the wise choice of many alternatives.

Willa A. Foster

CHAPTER OBJECTIVES

In this chapter, you will learn how to

- Define strategy.
- Create goals necessary for planning.
- Explain the importance of infrastructure.
- List examples of culture in the workplace.
- Explain and list examples of high-touch and low-touch customers.
- Express an understanding of consumption behavior.
- Use market segmentation to divide customers into serviceable groups.

Why a Strategy?

Excellent customer service is not an accident but the result of a well-thought-out plan.

The most important step toward achieving excellent customer service is developing a strategy. A **strategy** is a plan for positive action. A plan is always necessary when attempting to accomplish goals.

A strategy can help a business to determine the proper level of customer service. If too much customer service is provided, it may create a financial problem. If too little customer service is provided, customers may take their business elsewhere.

Several variables must be considered when developing a customer service strategy: planning, infrastructure, culture, high-touch and low-touch customers, consumption behavior, and market segmentation.

strategy A plan for positive action.

Planning

When undertaking the challenge of developing a comprehensive customer service strategy, planning is the first step. To begin the planning process, customer service providers must establish goals to determine what they would like to accomplish in their customer service.

Planning is, in a broad sense, finding a recognizable direction to focus on. More specifically, planning is the establishment of specific customer service goals. These goals may vary from reducing customer complaints to answering customer calls in 20 seconds or less. Establishing customer service goals will help customer service providers to define what they would like to accomplish. It is not uncommon for additional goals or priorities to surface as the strategy is being developed.

planning Finding a recognizable direction to focus on. More specifically, planning is the establishment of specific customer service goals.

"My dreams are worthless, my plans are dust, my goals are impossible. All are of no value unless they are followed by action. I will act now."
Og Mandino

Importance of Infrastructure

Customer service depends on the existence of an appropriate infrastructure. An **infrastructure** is made up of the networks of people, physical facilities, and information that support the production of customer service. Frequently, organizations attempt to implement customer service programs without considering the capabilities of their existing infrastructure. For example, if a company adds a toll-free customer service hotline and does not increase the number of telephone lines into its business, it may do more damage than good to its customer service reputation. While adding the toll-free line was an excellent idea, the lack of extra lines may cause customers to become frustrated and hang up before their questions or concerns have been addressed.

infrastructure Made up of the networks of people, physical facilities, and information that support the production of customer service.

One way of thinking of an infrastructure is that it is the "highway" that gets you where you need to go. Without a "highway," we do not always realize what is possible. Many cities find that if their infrastructures (water, sewer, roads, electricity, etc.) do not keep up with population growth or shifts, public services become inadequate. It is always interesting to see the new businesses that seem to pop up when a new road is built. In many cases, the need for those businesses already existed but, because the infrastructure was lacking, they did not open.

Infrastructures require a lot of planning. If future needs are not anticipated, future costs may be greater. Very few infrastructure investments show a positive return in less than three to five years. The infrastructure should meet the needs of the customer. The largest cost of producing great service is creating the infrastructure to support it.

Infrastructure must be used to its fullest potential. If current technology is in place but employees have not been trained to use it, it is wasted. Unfortunately, this is apparent in all too many businesses. Numerous voice mail systems, computers, copiers, software, and fax machines are never used because the people to whom they were made available were never trained on them or never made the commitment to initiate their use. Today's customers use technology and they expect their customer service providers to use it.

As sales grow, the company's ability to serve its customers' needs should also.

Culture

culture Composed of the values, beliefs, and norms shared by a group of people.

A customer service environment should have a customer service-oriented culture. **Culture** is composed of the values, beliefs, and norms shared by a group of people. Many people are not aware of the fact that every business has its own unique culture. All too often, management preaches the importance of positive customer service but then does not provide a work environment that allows that positive customer service to happen. If the "culture" does not encourage excellent customer service, excellent customer service will not exist.

Examples of Culture in Specific Industries

1. Typical workday hours
2. Industry lingo
3. Peer accountability
4. Levels of certification
5. Extra company-sponsored activities

Southwest Airlines is recognized as a service provider with few customer complaints and consistent on-time performance. This is largely due to the customer service culture that it creates for its employees. It encourages its employees to go above and beyond the call of duty. It allows its employees to dress comfortably yet professionally. Humor is an important part of the airline–customer relationship. Three ways that Southwest Airlines succeeds in creating a customer-friendly culture are as follows:

- **Practice the Golden Rule:** Do unto others as you would have them do unto you, both internally and externally.
- **View internal customers as number one:** Southwest believes that if you take care of the internal customers, they will automatically take care of the external customers.
- **Work hard, play hard:** Celebrate successes, offer incentives, and give people a reason to work hard.

High–Touch and Low–Touch Customers

There are many different types of customers and customer services. Depending on several variables, customers will have different customer service expectations. One method of understanding customers is to classify them as high-touch or low-touch customers. **High-touch customers** require a high level of customer interaction. These customers come into their customer service experience expecting a high level of service. In most cases, their perception is that the cost of providing the service is included in the price. If they do not experience a high level of interaction, they will probably be dissatisfied. The customer may not be capable of completing the interaction without assistance.

◀ **high–touch customers** Require a high level of customer interaction.

Examples of High Touch

1. Bank lobbies
2. Specialty stores
3. Hotel lobbies
4. Purchase of real estate
5. Lawyers and accountants
6. Prestige restaurant

When a choice is given, many customers will choose a low-touch experience and may even resent being required to participate in a high-touch experience. **Low-touch customers** expect a low level of customer interaction. Low touch frequently exists because of technology. It tends to have high usage and low cost per use.

◀ **low–touch customers** Expect a low level of customer interaction.

TEAM TIME

Sit down with your team and discuss the concept of *high-touch* and *low-touch* customers. Attempt to identify which group, high touch or low touch, represents the greatest percentage of your customers. Remember, the trend is for businesses to offer an increasing number of low-touch customer opportunities. Brainstorm with your group ideas as to methods of offering additional low-touch customer opportunities. Delete the ideas that are not feasible in your organization. Invite your supervisor to hear your ideas for creating new low-touch opportunities. He or she may not have considered all of the possibilities!

Examples of Low Touch

1. Pike passes (debit cards used on turnpikes)
2. Automatic teller machines
3. Express rental car checkout
4. Hotel bill viewing on television and express checkout
5. Pay-at-the-pump gasoline
6. Fast-food drive-up windows
7. Do-it-yourself copy shops
8. Online bill paying and account management
9. Self checkout
10. Downloading of music or ringtones

If customers are satisfied with and even expect a low-touch experience, it is inappropriate to require them to participate in a high-touch experience. Customers have many reasons for taking advantage of low-touch customer services. A mother with small children may choose to go to the drive-up window at her bank because it is much more convenient than unloading her children and going inside. If, upon arrival at the bank, she is told that her routine transaction must be completed inside, she may become discouraged and postpone completing it. If it happens often, she may change to a bank that will provide her with the conveniences that she requires.

◀ Consumption Behavior

◀ **consumption behavior** Refers to the customer's usage and payment patterns.

Consumption behavior refers to the customer's usage and payment patterns. Evaluating consumption behavior can be a relatively easy method of collecting information about a customer. This is especially true if the organization has an established method of customer data collection.

Most companies today have a computerized method of obtaining information about their customers' behavior patterns. Unfortunately, many do not know what to do with the information they have gathered. They have too much information that does not easily provide an improved understanding of the customer. Some of the important questions to ask when identifying consumption behavior are

- What are customers buying?
- Why did they buy it?
- Why did they buy more today than they did in our last interaction?
- Why did they call with a question?
- What was their question?
- How much did they buy?
- Have they bought from us before?
- How did they pay?
- When will they be installing/assembling the product?
- What else have they bought recently?

The more information an organization has about its customer's consumption patterns, the better prepared it is to create a strategy to better serve that customer. Most companies serve a variety of different customers with unique consumption patterns. It is not appropriate to serve all customers in exactly the same way. Companies that do so risk offending some customers, over-serving others, and neglecting others.

A guttering company had installed a top-of-the-line guttering material on a very expensive home. When the home was purchased, the new homeowners called the company to install some additional guttering. The company failed to show up on three different days that they were scheduled to do the installation. When they did arrive and completed the work, the homeowner was not home. No bill was left for the homeowner to pay. Three days later, an invoice was received by mail with the invoice date of the first scheduled installation day. The homeowner received the bill and placed it in the "to be paid" file. It was the homeowner's pattern to pay bills on a designated day during the week. The day after receiving the invoice, the homeowner received an angry phone call from the collections individual at the guttering company asking why the bill was not paid yet. The homeowner stated that the bill had just been received and would be paid within the next few days. The collections person then stated that all bills were to be paid cash on delivery.

When the homeowner explained that no bill was left after the work was completed and that the bill had just come in the mail, he was again told that the company did not look kindly on customers who failed to pay. The guttering company expected payment immediately or it would take action against the homeowner. The homeowner ended the phone call promising to send a check immediately and feeling upset at the fact that he had received the call in the first place. That evening (after the payment had been mailed), a neighbor stopped at the homeowner's house to compliment his unique gutters and ask who had installed them. The homeowner shared the story and also stated that no matter how attractive the guttering was, he would never recommend the company to anyone else.

On the surface, this sounds like just a griping customer story about an unglamorous home improvement product. The reality is that many businesses generate all of their revenue selling products or services that are not extremely exciting. This company could have preserved its reputation and possibly retained a potentially influential customer by examining the customer's consumption behavior and improving its method of collecting on unpaid accounts.

Too many companies end up hurting their business opportunities because they do not consider their customers' consumption behavior. How many times have you seen a company advertise or at least list on a product box or installation instructions that it has a free customer help line, only to attempt to call the number and then find out that the help line is available only from Monday through Friday 8:00 a.m. to 5:00 p.m. Eastern time? Does anyone have a problem with his lawn mower during other hours or attempt to install software on her home computers at other times? Identifying consumption behavior of specific customers can enable an organization to most effectively serve the customers when, where, and how they need it.

"Go the extra mile. It's never crowded."
Unknown

◖ Segmentation of Your Market

◖ **market segmentation**
Dividing customers into groups with similar characteristics.

Understanding your customers' similarities is important when developing a customer service strategy. **Market segmentation** is dividing customers into groups with similar characteristics.

Segmentation will help to divide customers into serviceable groups, making it easier to assess the appropriate services to provide. Segmentation can also identify unique customer groups with special needs, such as health clubs with babysitting services or eye care clinics with available customer transportation.

Segmentation can also identify common and less common customer service needs. Segmentation is often difficult because of customer diversity, but it is an excellent starting point when developing a strategy.

Sample Customer Service Segments

1. Types of service needed or desired
2. Similarities among your current customers

3. Peak hours of your business and the specific customers doing business at those times
4. The amount of service desired
5. Creation of your own segments that are appropriate to your product or service

Development of a Strategy

When the variables—planning, infrastructure, culture, high- and low-touch customers, consumption behavior, and market segmentation—have been evaluated, it is time to create a customer service strategy.

The following seven guidelines provide a guide for creating the strategy:

1. **Segment your customers:** Divide them into groups with similar characteristics.
2. **Identify the largest and most profitable customer groups:** Initially, it is better to serve the largest customer group, representing the majority of your business.
3. **Determine your customers' expectations:** Find out what your customers want from their experience with you.
4. **Develop a plan to achieve their expectations efficiently:** Create an innovative strategy that will allow you to serve your customers effectively.
5. **Implement the plan:** Put your new strategy into practice, implementing all aspects of the strategy at the same time.
6. **Set an evaluation timetable:** Before implementing your strategy, determine when an evaluation of its success will be conducted.
7. **Evaluate and continue to improve the strategy:** Evaluate the effectiveness of the new customer service strategy and make appropriate improvements. Keep making changes to keep the new strategy as current as possible.

Job Link

Make a list of some of the market segments of which you are a part. Try to list as many as 25 different segments to which you have a connection. Notice how diverse the segments are and how similar and dissimilar the other individuals in each of the segments are to you. Apply your new awareness of the diversity of market segments the next time you are segmenting your own customer groups.

KEY TERMS

consumption behavior

culture

high-touch customers

infrastructure

low-touch customers

market segmentation

planning

strategy

QUICK QUIZ

1. A strategy is a plan for positive action.   T or F
2. By establishing customer service goals, customer service providers define what they would like to accomplish.   T or F
3. Infrastructure investments usually have an immediate payback.   T or F
4. The values, beliefs, and norms shared by a group of people are their personality.   T or F
5. Bank lobbies, specialty stores, hotel lobbies, lawyers, and accountants are all examples of low-touch customer encounters.   T or F
6. Low touch frequently exists because of technology.   T or F
7. Online bill paying is growing in popularity as a low-touch customer opportunity.   T or F
8. Consumption behavior is irrelevant and difficult information to collect.   T or F
9. Market segmentation is dividing customers into groups with similar characteristics. T or F
10. Setting an evaluation timetable is one of the guidelines for developing a strategy.   T or F

OPPORTUNITIES FOR CRITICAL THINKING

1. Explain market segmentation.
2. Define culture and give two examples of culture in the workplace.
3. Explain the difference between high-touch and low-touch environments.
4. What variables should be considered when developing a customer service strategy?
5. Look for examples of infrastructure in your own organization.
6. Contrast the potential success of a strategy that is developed according to the guidelines for creating a strategy and one that is not.
7. Identify some customer service market segments that you are in.
8. Give examples of situations where high-touch and low-touch environments are appropriate.
9. What role do customers' expectations play in the establishment of customer service strategy?
10. Examine the culture of your own workplace.

SKILL BUILDING

Time Management

Time management is necessary for anyone who deals with customers. No one can improve your time management skills but you. If we have not done an effective job of managing our time, we will be more likely to become frustrated and to take our frustrations out on our customers. It is easy to let time slip away or to allow one customer to take the amount of time that would ordinarily be divided among several.

Time management must be ongoing and regularly practiced to make it a way of life. Here are ten tips for better time management:

1. Set goals and determine their priority.
2. Keep an updated calendar handy at all times.
3. Set tentative deadlines and reward yourself for meeting them.
4. Make a to-do list for the next day before you go to bed at night!
5. Take a break!
6. Focus on what must be accomplished.
7. Work *smart*—not *hard.*
8. Use the Swiss cheese method. (Break tasks into smaller pieces and work on them a little at a time.)
9. Evaluate. (Determine what is taking all of your time.)
10. Reward yourself for time well managed.

To evaluate your own time management, complete the following exercise:

For three to five days, keep a log of how your time is spent. Record your activities, phone calls, breaks, and so on in accurate time intervals. Be honest about the time that you spend on all activities. Also, record whether the time was spent on a professional or personal activity. Analyze the amounts of time that you have spent on all of your different activities.

Sample Time Log					
START TIME	STOP TIME	ELAPSED TIME	ACTIVITY CODE	ACTIVITY DESCRIPTION	COMMENTS

Activity Codes
Work-Specific Tasks—WST
Work-General Tasks—WGT
Personal-Productive—PP
Personal-Nonproductive—PNP
Miscellaneous—MISC

Divide the time spent into five categories: work-specific tasks, work-general tasks, personal-productive, personal-nonproductive, and miscellaneous. Also include any comments that would clarify your activity or that you believe are pertinent.

After tallying how your time was spent, attempt to draw conclusions about how you are spending your time. If more than 20 percent of your time at work is being spent on personal activities or 20 percent of your time at home is being spent on work activities, it may indicate that you are allowing each to spill over to the other.

Sometimes the conclusion that we draw from keeping a time log is that unimportant activities are taking the majority of our time. Time management is an ongoing process. Try to use your time more appropriately; you may be surprised at the result.

If possible, share your time log with at least one other person. Ask those you share it with to suggest ways that you could better manage your time. Other people's ideas on how we can better manage our time can be helpful because we learn from their experiences.

Ethics in Action

Your coworker has been arriving back at their workstation late following their lunch break for the last few weeks. Your department is evaluated on a departmental basis. Your coworker's tardiness is bringing down productivity, which could put the entire group's efficiency rating in jeopardy. Some others in the group are becoming angry and are about to report the tardy employee. What would you do?

CHALLENGE ## Departmental Factoid

One of the unique aspects of life in any professional environment is the specialized terminology that is used to communicate within departments and institutions. Unfortunately, this unique terminology is frequently learned the hard way through individuals questioning what a certain word or abbreviation means. Customers, both internal and external, may have a difficult time knowing the meaning of specialized terms. This specialized terminology is commonly called a *departmental factoid*.

Challenge Objectives

1. To demonstrate an understanding of what a departmental factoid is.
2. To create a list of unique terminology used to communicate within an organization.
3. To learn to create an attractive brochure that is informational and easy to read.

Assignment

Create a list of departmental factoids that would help your customers to better understand how to speak the language of your specific area. Good candidates to be included on your list are those words that you find yourself frequently defining or those that you had to seek an explanation for when you began working in your specific department or industry.

Presentation

Present your list of departmental factoids with definitions in the form of an informational brochure. Your brochure should include the following:

1. Cover page with title and graphic
2. Attractive layout detailing your factoids and their definitions
3. Methodical arrangement of factoids (alphabetical, numerical, etc.)
4. Helpful hints for the reader to remember the specific factoids
5. Professional appearance
6. Easy to read

A successful brochure is not only attractive but also informational. In the business world, the production of brochures can be costly if they are not well designed and useful.

■ **Helpful Hint:** Take this opportunity to try Microsoft® PowerPoint® or similar publishing software. Several are available, and they can make an ordinary sheet of facts into a very attractive and readable document with minimal effort—one more beneficial skill to add to your professional resume!

ANSWERS TO QUICK QUIZ

1. T	5. F	9. T
2. T	6. T	10. T
3. F	7. T	
4. F	8. F	

Empowerment

From Chapter 5 of *Customer Service: A Practical Approach*. Sixth Edition. Elaine K. Harris. Copyright © 2013 by Pearson Education, Inc. All rights reserved.

Empowerment

Remember This

Creative thinking may mean the realization that there's no particular virtue in doing things the way they have always been done.

Roger Van Oeck

CHAPTER OBJECTIVES

In this chapter, you will learn how to

- List examples of empowerment.
- Explain the importance of a mission and purpose statement.
- Define coproduction and self-sufficiency.
- Create coproduction examples within your own company.
- Discuss the importance of a well-designed customer service system.

What Is Empowerment?

As businesses struggle to retain their current customers and to attract new ones, management is required to look beyond traditional approaches. One new approach that has significant implications in the customer service industry is the idea of empowerment.

In customer service, **empowerment** is to enable or permit customer service providers to make a range of decisions to assist their customers. Customer service providers are continuously faced with customer situations that are unique to the customer and that are somewhere beyond the boundaries of the existing policies. Through empowerment, customer service providers are given the discretion to make decisions to further assist their customers.

Empowerment allows customer service providers to decide on their own whether or not customers' requests should be granted. Frequently, when customers have contacted a company with an inquiry, they have fully explained their situation to the person who is handling their call. If providers are truly empowered, they can, within limits, decide how to resolve the situation. If the providers have to put the customers on hold or make them wait for an answer while the situation is explained to a supervisor, everyone loses. The customers have to wait or possibly retell their stories, the providers are taken away from their regular duties feeling like helpless middlemen, and the supervisor has to hear a hurried explanation of the situation. This scenario could be avoided through empowerment.

empowerment To enable or permit customer service providers to make a range of decisions to assist their customers.

Importance of a Mission and Purpose Statement

Empowerment is a philosophy that must be reflected in the culture of a business. The culture is composed of the values, beliefs, and norms shared by a group of people. In an "empowered culture," employees know the range of their power. They have been trained in the range of possible solutions to questions, and they know that their superiors are willing to live with their decisions.

All businesses that deal with customers should have an official mission and purpose statement. This statement expresses the **purpose**—the reason for the organization's existence—and the **mission**—the means by which the organization will fulfill its purpose.

purpose The reason for an organization's existence.

mission The means by which the organization will fulfill its purpose.

Empowerment = Opportunity

Empowerment is a true opportunity. Customer service providers who deal with a large number of customers frequently know the solution to most common questions and problems. If they are given the power to deal directly with some of the more routine issues, more time is available for them to handle the more unique situations and to be thorough with all of their customers. Empowerment also frees the time of supervisors who may otherwise be less productive because they have to deal with issues that could be handled more quickly by the customer service providers.

Job Link

Take a minute to write down your own personal purpose statement. Why do you exist? Write your statement down on a card and place it where you can see it often. Do your priorities fit your purpose?

Examples of Empowerment

At a local bank, all bank tellers are given $100 each month to distribute among their customers. This money is allocated to be used to compensate customers for being inconvenienced, for errors, or for having an especially long wait. The tellers can use this money as they deem appropriate. They can send the customers flowers, buy a steak dinner or tickets to a baseball game, or perform other goodwill gestures. The employees may not give any money or gifts to members of their families. They must document on an official form whom the gifts were given to and why. The employees know that at any time the bank customer may be contacted to confirm the donation.

Some utility companies are empowering their customer service providers by giving them the opportunity to hear a customer's situation and then to grant that customer special payment arrangement that will better meet the customer's current financial needs. The employees are also encouraged to send four cards to the customers of their choice each day. These cards may recall something that the customer shared with the customer service provider like the birth of a new baby or the purchase of a new home. The cards may also say "congratulations," "just a note," or "oops—we made a mistake." The intent is to create relationships with the customers, so that they feel as though they have a real link with a person within the company.

"Those who bring sunshine into the lives of others cannot keep it from themselves."
James M. Barrie

Steps to Empowering Customer Service Providers

Empowerment does not just happen. It is the result of a company's focused efforts to establish guidelines, train employees, accept consequences, and celebrate positive results. When creating an empowerment program within your organization, consider the following recommendations:

1. **Paint a picture of what you hope to accomplish:** This "picture" can be an inspiring reminder of what your organization is trying to accomplish and how it can benefit each member of the organization.
2. **Allow workers to own their empowerment choices:** Give them responsibility they can handle and give them feedback on their choices. Do not punish when mistakes occur, but instead retrain. Employees will avoid taking empowerment chances if they fear repercussions.
3. **Reward and recognize positive examples and results of empowerment:** You will show those in your organization that you are committed to the empowerment process.
4. **Commit for the long haul:** Positive results will not necessarily appear overnight, but they will be worth the wait!

Coproduction of Customer Service

Another way of thinking of empowerment in customer service is to empower the customer. **Coproduction** occurs when customers participate in providing at least a part of their own service. Customers are often willing and interested in participating in the customer service process.

◀ coproduction
When customers participate in providing at least a part of their own customer service.

Examples of Coproduction

1. Salad bars (make your own salad as you like it)
2. Free beverage refills that you get yourself
3. Self-service copy shops
4. Parents' ability to check their children's grades online
5. College self-advisement (create your own schedule)
6. Completion of medical and insurance information while waiting for the doctor
7. Availability of your account number or medical chart number
8. Requests that deposit slips be completed before going through the bank line and providing a place for customers to fill them out
9. Telephone customer assistance lines
10. Payment at the pump for gasoline

A customer service system should be designed so that customers are allowed and encouraged to provide their own customer service. If everything else is equal, a system produces service more effectively when the customers participate as much as they can.

"When was honey ever made with one bee hive?"
Thomas Hood

Included in the concept of coproduction is customer self-sufficiency. **Self-sufficiency** happens when customers use systems in place to meet

■ self-sufficiency
Customers using
systems in place to
meet their own service
needs at a level that
results in satisfaction.

their own service needs at a level that results in satisfaction. As the market has evolved, customers have become willing participants in the provision of their own customer service. Observant businesses have put, or are in the process of putting, in place the tools for customers to successfully achieve their desired level of customer service. Some of these tools include:

- Self checkout
- "Build your own anything"
- Online warranties
- Instructions
- How-to videos
- Automatically texted available bank balances
- Online bill paying
- Shipping tracking information
- Prescription fulfillment via bar code scanning

The main difference between coproduction and self-sufficiency is that coproduction usually takes place at a designated time (i.e., paperwork filled out in the doctor's office while waiting for an appointment) and self-sufficiency is available when and where the customer the customer wishes to access it. Self-sufficiency strives to give the customer additional independence. A customer using an appliance that needs to see the owner's manual is more likely to go to their computer to search for it online than they are to dig out an old file of owner's manuals from their desk drawer. Hopefully they will find the manual quickly and have their question answered. In the attempt to address this emerging trend, a photographic supply company in Texas no longer includes warranties or instructions with their products. Instead they e-mail, at the time of their purchase, the customers a link to obtain it online and then post all of the information at their product site, so that a simple search will result in the customers finding the information. Their customers have been pleased with this simple change in the way that this company works to serve them. When customers can experience positive customer service when and where they desire it, their level of satisfaction will increase.

■ Why Coproduction Works

Coproduction works because when customers participate in the process, they have some degree of ownership of the situation. In a manner of speaking, they have contributed to its success. Coproduction also works because customers are not only contributing to the customer service experience but also staying occupied instead of feeling that they are waiting endlessly or being imposed on. In addition, customer service providers have someone who is sharing the work and responsibility; they are therefore less stressed in successfully performing their jobs.

Coproduction is not about making the customer do all of the work. It is, instead, about creating a partnership. Coproduction is not about abandoning your customers, being unwilling to assist, or letting the blind lead the blind. If a system is designed for coproduction but some element of the process is not in place, the system will fail. A business that requires the customer to fill out an order form in a store to complete a sale but that does not have pencils or order forms available will not succeed in empowering the customer. In this instance, coproduction cannot succeed.

Coproduction is not appropriate in every customer service situation or for every customer. In a prestige environment, it is inappropriate to expect that the customer will automatically want to participate in providing customer service. The customers may believe that they have paid (or are going to pay) someone else to do it.

The following are some techniques to help customers become better coproducers:

- **Ask telephone callers to be prepared:** Have you ever wondered why you are placed on hold when calling in a mail order purchase and then a pleasant voice reminds you to have your catalog and credit card handy? The company is very subtly reminding you to be a coproducer.
- **Repeat important information:** Asking customers to confirm their drive-up window orders allows mistakes to be corrected and customers to rethink their choices if they have a change to make.
- **Train customers to be coproducers:** Provide little things like simple instructions on a form to be completed, prominently displayed signs indicating "express lanes" in discount stores, handing menus to customers who are waiting to be seated in restaurants, cart return areas in parking lots (along with a sign thanking customers for the cart return), and so on. When customers know what you expect of them, they can assist you more quickly and efficiently.
- **Tell customers why they should want to be coproducers:** If customers understand how everyone involved benefits from coproduction, they are more likely to participate enthusiastically.

TEAM TIME

Sit down with your team and discuss the concept of coproduction. Remember, *coproduction occurs when customers participate in providing at least part of their own service.* Create a new method of coproduction for your department. Coproduction should be a positive asset to the customer service experience. Make the process simple and easily explained. Test the new method of coproduction; and, if it passes your review, share your concept with a supervisor. The supervisor will likely be impressed with the initiative of your team! Way to go!

Design of Systems

customer service system Any set of procedures that contributes to the completion of customer service.

Empowerment and coproduction are two facets of customer service that do not happen automatically. They must be carefully included in a customer service system. A **customer service system** is any set of procedures that contributes to the completion of customer service. Not all customer service systems work efficiently and effectively. They must be designed to do so.

Unfortunately, many systems are in place because sometime in the past someone decided that a situation would be handled a certain way, and no one has ever updated the procedure. Frequently, the person who has created a system is not the person who has to work with it. The best person in an organization to participate in creating a new system is the person who deals with it on an ongoing basis and who can see "the big picture."

If a question is repeatedly asked or a process has more than a few steps, a system update may be needed.

Guidelines for System Design

The following six guidelines will help to create an effective customer service system:

1. **Identify:** an area in need of a new procedure or a system update.
2. **List:** the steps necessary to create or improve the system.
3. **Review:** the mission and purpose statement to make sure that you stay on track with the company's goals.
4. **Seek to empower:** those involved, both providers and customers. Eliminate unnecessary steps.
5. **Create a culture:** that supports empowerment.
6. **Evaluate the system's effectiveness:** after it has been in operation for a specified period of time. "Those who bring sunshine into the lives of others cannot keep it from themselves."

KEY TERMS

coproduction	customer service system	mission
self-sufficiency	empowerment	purpose

QUICK QUIZ

1. Empowerment is to enable or permit customer service providers to make a range of decisions to assist their customers.   T or F
2. In an "empowered culture," employees are unclear as to the range of their power.   T or F
3. The reason an organization exists is its purpose.   T or F
4. Coproduction is when the customers participate in providing at least a part of their own service.   T or F

5. Self-checkout lanes in stores are controversial examples of coproduction.   T or F
6. Coproduction means that customers do the majority of the work in a customer interaction.   T or F
7. A set of procedures that contributes to the completion of customer service is a system. T or F

8. The best person to help to create a system is frequently the person who deals with it on an ongoing basis.   T or F
9. Systems are applicable in a wide variety of areas in business and in life.   T or F
10. Creating a culture that supports empowerment is an important part of creating a successful customer service system.   T or F

OPPORTUNITIES FOR CRITICAL THINKING

1. List three examples of coproduction. How do coproduction and self-sufficiency differ?
2. What are some guidelines for creating an effective customer service system?
3. How can updating a system or creating a new system enhance the provision of excellent customer service?
4. What are some types of businesses that are the most conducive to coproduction?
5. Write a mission and purpose statement for your department or class.
6. Explain empowerment.
7. How can a lack of empowerment affect a customer service provider's ability to provide the service that customers expect?
8. Why are so many ineffective systems in place in organizations?
9. In your experience, are customers willing to provide a part of their own service? Why or why not?
10. Why are individuals sometimes resistant to new systems?

SKILL BUILDING

Creating Coproduction

Most organizations can meet a customer's basic needs. To be truly successful in the future, organizations must create an environment in which customer service is proactive and not mandatorily reactive. In a coproductive environment, customers are allowed and encouraged to participate in providing at least a part of their own service.

Some of the requirements of coproduction are

◀ Coproduction must create a partnership between the customer and the provider.
◀ Customers must have available the tools necessary to coproduce.

◀ Customers must know what their role in coproduction is.

List some ways that you could create coproduction in your own organization.

◀
◀
◀
◀
◀

Share your new ideas for coproduction with your coworkers or small group. Strive to sell others on the positive benefits of creating coproduction!

Ethics in Action

You work at a very popular video rental store. You have a great relationship with your customers and have gotten to know them all personally. When they come in, they look for you and seem to think of you as a friend. Today one of your favorite customers came in. She was very upset because she had received a letter from your company informing her that her account would be charged for a video that she never had returned. She is on a limited income and said that she could not afford to pay for the movie. She didn't even remember the movie and cannot find it. She came to you because you are her "friend." She has requested that you waive the fee for the movie. This is against company policy but you hate to disappoint any customer. What should you do? One more thing to know, after she left you looked at her account. Sadly, this is not the first time that she has made this mistake.

CHALLENGE Design of a New System

Customer service is more likely to occur when a well-designed customer service system is in place. Since many customer service systems are outdated or were created by individuals unfamiliar with the unique characteristics of a situation, a system update or review may be necessary. By learning how to create an effective customer service system, customer service providers are equipping themselves with the ability to initiate and request change.

Challenge Objectives

1. To demonstrate an understanding of how systems can affect the success of a customer service program.
2. To implement the students' ideas in their own work environments (contingent on their supervisors' approval).
3. To successfully present to others the system developed.

Assignment

Observe your work or personal environment. Attempt to identify an area of confusion or disorganization or a system that in your opinion is just not working as well as it could. Once you have identified this area, attempt to design an improved system to handle the challenge more effectively. Your system should include the steps necessary to better deal with the situation. Review the guidelines for creating an effective customer service system for additional guidance as you create your system. Also include a list of those who will be participating in the implementation of the new system.

Presentation

Present your newly designed system in the form of a proposal. Include in your proposal

1. A cover letter or memorandum introducing your proposal
2. Explanation of the current system or the lack of system
3. Reasons why a system update is needed
4. How the new system will improve efficiency
5. How much you estimate it will cost to implement

6. How you will train those affected by the new system to implement it
7. An explanation of the system itself
8. Visual aids that further illustrate the system
9. A summary paragraph that expresses the key aspects of the proposed system

The success of your proposal will not depend on how intricate the system itself is, but instead on how well it is designed and how well you express your ideas on paper and communicate in written form.

◀ **Helpful Hint:** Take this opportunity to create a Microsoft® PowerPoint® presentation to share your proposal. If you have not previously worked with PowerPoint,® ask a friend to help or just jump in. It is an easy-to-learn program and will greatly enhance your professionalism.

ANSWERS TO QUICK QUIZ

1. T	5. T	9. T
2. F	6. F	10. T
3. T	7. T	
4. T	8. T	

Communications in Customer Service

Communications in Customer Service

Remember This

Obstacles are those frightful things you see when you take your eyes off your goals.

Unknown

CHAPTER OBJECTIVES

In this chapter, you will learn how to

- Explain the relationship between communication and customer service.
- Define customer intelligence.
- Discuss the benefits of relationship marketing.
- List the five main methods of communication.
- Demonstrate the use of voice inflection to positively convey information.
- Create your own words to use/words to avoid.

What Is Communication?

Customer service requires the ability to communicate effectively. **Communication** is the process in which information, ideas, and understanding are shared between two (or more) people. Frequently, individuals think that they are communicating, but the element of understanding may not be taking place. Customer service providers must develop their communication skills so that they are proficient in all methods of communication.

◀ communication
The process in which information, ideas, and understanding are shared between two (or more) people.

Building Customer Intelligence

The challenge of communicating effectively is made more difficult when providers do not have a good understanding of who their customer really is. One way to develop a more intimate understanding of customers is to build customer intelligence. **Customer intelligence** is the process of gathering information; building a historical database; and developing an understanding of current, potential, and lapsed customers. Customer intelligence or a customer IQ allows organizations, specifically customer service providers, to better serve customer groups. It can help businesses to appropriately tailor services and service approaches to specific customers. Most business people today have recognized the importance of identifying why customers are more loyal to one organization than to others offering similar service or product opportunities. Customers are participating in the collection of customer intelligence more today than any time in history.

◀ customer intelligence The process of gathering information; building a historical database; and developing an understanding of current, potential, and lapsed customers.

For years, businesses have attempted to identify the best method of rewarding customers for their business and loyalty. Many businesses have found an excellent method of doing so and of collecting customer intelligence in the process. Targeted reward programs offer customers the opportunity to sign up for various types of rewards. This can be an accurate method of tracking customer purchases and of rewarding customers for their loyalty. CVS, American Eagle, JC Penney, numerous hotel chains, and many other companies have been successful with this strategy. They can collect pertinent information while enticing the customer to come back and make additional purchases and take advantage of further services. The customers feel good about their savings and the company can continue to collect purchasing information. The most important benefit may be that the customers feel like the company appreciates their business. As a company is developing customer intelligence, it must strive to obtain a true picture of the customer. Examining only selected areas of customer information can result in a fragmented view of customers. In this instance, no information would be better than inaccurate information.

Customer intelligence can enhance the possibility of improved relationship marketing. **Relationship marketing** is cultivating a lasting and mutually beneficial connection with customers. Many businesses

◀ relationship marketing
Cultivating a lasting and mutually beneficial connection with customers.

already have a considerable amount of information about customers at their disposal; they just have not recognized what can be interpreted from customer data. The methods by which customers choose to conduct business; the time of day they have questions; and the depth of their expected interactions, purchasing patterns, expectations, and much more fall into the realm of customer intelligence. As with any personal or business relationship, the more we get to know and understand others, the better we can communicate with them. The more positively and appropriately we approach our communication efforts with customers, the more likely that we will succeed in effectively serving our customers.

Customer intelligence takes market segmentation a step further. *a\ Market segmentation means dividing customers into groups with shared characteristics*; customer intelligence examines not just today's customers but also lapsed customers. Finally, customer intelligence is continually being developed and added to as new information or trends are discovered.

◀ **listening** The ability to hear and understand what the speaker is saying.

◀ **writing** Communicating by using the written word so that others can understand the intended message.

◀ **talking** Speaking, using words and terminology that others can comprehend.

◀ **reading** The ability to look at and comprehend the written word.

◀ **nonverbal expression** Tone and inflection of voice, facial expressions, posture, and eye contact. Nonverbal communication can contradict the message conveyed through another method of communication.

◀ Methods of Communication

Five main methods of communication are used in effective customer service interaction.

1. **Listening:** The ability to hear and understand what the speaker is saying.
2. **Writing:** Communicating by using the written word so that others can understand the intended message.
3. **Talking:** Speaking, using words and terminology that others can comprehend.
4. **Reading:** The ability to look at and comprehend the written word.
5. **Nonverbal expression:** Tone and inflection of voice, facial expressions, posture, and eye contact. Nonverbal communication can contradict the message conveyed through another method of communication.

All methods of communication are used in customer service. Customer service providers must continue to improve their communication skills. Different environments place greater emphasis on different methods of communication, but listening is thought by many to be the most important method of communication.

◀ Listening

"Learn to listen. Opportunity could be knocking at your door very softly."
Frank Tyger

To listen to your customers is to show them that you care about and respect their questions and concerns. It is not easy to be a good listener; it takes practice and dedication to improve your listening techniques. Listening is a skill that must continuously be developed.

Several barriers to good listening exist. A listener may be distracted from what is being said, may have a closed mind to the speaker and the message, may not stop talking, or may be lazy and unwilling to make the commitment to be a good listener.

Many people believe that we have shorter attention spans because of the visual environment in which we live. We have become so accustomed to commercial interruptions and the pause button on our remote that we find it difficult to pay attention to a speaker without allowing our minds to drift to other things. The best way to keep your mind focused on the speaker and to avoid becoming distracted is to pay attention. We can think about 10 times faster than we can speak, so frequently we have processed what speakers have said and are waiting for them to catch up with us. By focusing on speakers and on what is being said, we are less likely to miss the messages being delivered.

We must also avoid becoming visually distracted. The clock on the wall, the cut on your finger, what is happening in the hallway, and your daily To-Do List are all tempting diversions. Visual distractions may be very appealing because they require little effort to receive and may promote new ideas and thoughts, all of which take away from our ability to really hear what is being said.

The closed mind is a tremendous challenge to listening. No human being is without ideas, beliefs, and values. Those things that we think and believe may prevent us from really hearing what someone is saying. A good listener must consider what is being said and avoid jumping to conclusions. When we open our minds to new ideas, we have the opportunity to learn new things and to hear different perspectives.

Listening requires the listener to stop talking and to hear what the speaker is saying. It is not uncommon for communication problems to arise when the speaker is trying to convey the situation but the listener interrupts before the speaker is finished. It has been said that humans were given two ears and one mouth because we are supposed to listen twice as much as we speak. Putting that into practice is not as easy as it sounds. When listening to someone, allow the speaker to complete the thought before giving your response. Be an observer. Watch for pauses in the speaker's delivery that may indicate that the speaker is finished speaking. Also, wait until the speaker has stopped talking before you determine your response.

A good listener

1. Conveys sincerity
2. Does not interject his or her own thoughts
3. Nods head
4. Does not finish the sentence for the speaker
5. Paraphrases what was said
6. Leans toward the speaker
7. Shares positive comments
8. Shows good eye contact

Practice good listening skills. The next time a coworker stops to talk with you, practice good listening skills. Look him or her in the eye, nod your head, let the person finish his or her sentences, and repeat what was said to you. Your coworker will think that you cared about what he or she was saying, and you will be practicing an effective customer service tool. Give it a try!

To improve your listening skills, try the following:

1. Focus on the speaker and what he or she is saying.
2. Look at the speaker and make eye contact when possible. If you are listening on the telephone, make notes as you listen.
3. Listen with an open mind.
4. Rephrase what was said to clarify that you understood the intended message.
5. Control your body language. Do not show impatience or disapproval.

A good listener knows the joy of sharing and communicating with others. Work to become the best listener you can be.

◀ Voice Inflection as a Customer Service Tool

◀ **voice inflection**
A variation in the pitch, timing, or loudness of the voice.

◀ **pitch** The highs and lows of the voice.

Many communicators have a hard time conveying their spoken message to others. If others frequently ask you to repeat what you said, cut you off before you are finished speaking, or do not take you seriously, the problem may be the way you use your voice. **Voice inflection** is a variation in the pitch, timing, or loudness of the voice. **Pitch** is the highs and lows of the voice. A national study has shown that some of the most unpleasant voice characteristics of Americans are talking in a whining, complaining, or nagging tone; a high-pitched, squeaky voice; a loud, grating voice; mumbling; and talking too fast. Vocal problems are amplified by the telephone. Your voice and message reveal some very important characteristics about the person you are.

Some of the characteristics revealed are

- Level of job satisfaction
- Attitude
- Gender
- Education
- Knowledge level
- Speed that you work and react
- Confidence

◀ The part of the country you are from
◀ Status
◀ Energy level
◀ Mood

Many people believe that our voices reflect our personalities. To illustrate the power of voice inflection, try the following exercise. Read the following sentence in your normal voice:

John solved the software problem.

Repeat the sentence as a question, then as a secret, and then with surprise. The message conveyed using different voice inflection should have been different each time it was read. The voice inflection that we use can send different messages depending on where we place emphasis.

To improve your voice inflection, try the following:

1. Tape yourself.
2. Ask friends for their honest assistance.
3. Make a conscious effort to improve.
4. Keep listening to yourself. It is easy to slip back into old habits. Excellent voice inflection takes practice!

◀ Telephones and Customer Service

When you are on the telephone, you are selling yourself. A large percentage of customer service interaction takes place by phone. Due to this fact, customer service providers must have outstanding telephone skills. When communicating with customers by phone, the advantages of face-to-face communication do not exist because there are no visual aids or body language. Instead, the communicator must depend on the listening skills, the ability to respond effectively to questions, and voice inflection.

The following are seven steps to answering a call successfully:

1. *Smile!* Your voice will sound friendlier if you have a smile on your face!
2. Answer the call with an *enthusiastic and professional greeting.* Your entire organization is depending on you to make a positive first impression.
   • Greet the caller.
   • Identify your organization or department.
   • Introduce yourself.
   • Offer your assistance.
3. *Ask questions* about anything that is not clear to you. If additional information is needed, ask for it and explain why it is needed.

4. *Give answers and assistance as quickly as possible.* If you cannot solve the problem or answer the question, let the customer know what will happen next.
5. *Thank the caller.* Ask if you may be of further assistance.
6. *Conclude the call in a positive manner.* Think of every call as the beginning of a new relationship.
7. *Follow up on the call* to make sure that the customer is pleased with the result and to make sure that everything you promised was delivered.

Organization is crucial when you interact with customers on the telephone. To become more organized, consider the following:

- Always have a notepad available. This is handy for making notes and jotting down the customer's name.
- Know the company's policies or have a reference close by.
- Tell the customer your name.
- Practice great listening skills.
- Check back with the customer to ensure that something was really completed.

Words to Use/Words to Avoid

When dealing with customers, some words are more positive and appropriate to use. Many of us use very negative and demeaning words when we speak with others. If we interact with customers, we must rework our vocabulary so that we use words to create a positive environment.

Some customer service providers find it helpful to list Words to Use/Words to Avoid on a card so that it is available for easy reference.

TEAM TIME

Sit down with your team and discuss the concept of *Words to Use/Words to Avoid.* Within your team, create your own list of 10 words to use and 10 words to avoid. Customize your words to fit your specific business. Consider the customers that you serve as you choose your words. When your list is completed, duplicate the list and have each team member strive to use or avoid the words. In two weeks, meet with your team again and discuss how effective or ineffective the words have been as you have dealt with customers. Hopefully you will find that you are having more word success with your customers due to better word choices.

Words to Use	Words to Avoid
Please	Can't
Yes	Never
May I	Don't
Consider this	You have to
Do	Don't tell me no
Let's negotiate	Won't
Will	Not our policy
Thank you	Not my job
You	Profanity
Us	Vulgarity
Appreciate	Problem
Can	Sorry
Use customer's name	Love slang (honey, etc.)
Would you like	We'll try
Opportunity	Haven't had time
Challenge	I don't know
Regret	Hang on for a second

Power Phrases

By using power phrases, we can send the message to our customers that they are very important and that we value their opinions. Here are 10 examples of power phrases:

1. Due to your specialized knowledge.
2. What a unique suggestion!
3. I'd like your considered opinion.
4. Please.
5. You are absolutely right!
6. If I could borrow just a moment of your time.
7. May I?
8. As you, of course, know.
9. I'd like your advice.
10. I would appreciate it if.

Using power phrases in our conversations with customers can express to them that their ideas are important. We can also let them know that we recognize the value of their time and expertise.

Power of Eye Contact

Eye contact is always important when we are communicating with others. **Eye contact** is allowing our eyes to make visual contact with someone else's eyes. In our culture, eye contact conveys sincerity and interest. Avoiding eye contact may suggest a lack of concern or lack of honesty. Our eyes can also convey compassion and caring. Customers may perceive that a customer service provider is not interested in what they are saying if they do not periodically make eye contact with the customer.

Even when a customer service provider deals with customers by telephone, he or she must be concerned with eye contact because of interaction with internal customers.

When dealing with people from other cultures, customer service providers should be aware of cultural differences. In many other cultures, eye avoidance is a sign of respect. Be sensitive to others, but use eye contact whenever possible.

Appeal to the Senses in Communication

When attempting to communicate with customers, it is helpful to appeal to as many senses as is possible. A waiter in a restaurant can create a dramatic picture of a food item if he describes it vividly for you and then shows it to you. He is appealing to your senses of sound, sight, and possibly smell. The combination creates more impact than appealing to just one of the senses. An example of this in customer service is when a customer has brought in a bill that he or she believes is incorrect; it would be helpful to show the customer the billing method and to describe how the bill was determined. The more senses we appeal to, the greater the possibility that customers will understand our message.

When customer service providers work exclusively on the telephone, they may appeal to additional senses not only by clearly explaining to the customer the answer to their concern but also by providing written documentation of what was discussed. This documentation could be e-mailed or mailed as a follow-up to the phone conversation.

Communication and Technology

The customer service industry has been greatly impacted and enhanced by technological advances. Customer service providers must familiarize themselves with the technological opportunities that they have available to them. Six main areas of technology have emerged as being important to the customer service industry. The Internet, e-mail, automated phone systems, voice mail, fax machines, and texting are actively in use on a daily basis. Customer service providers must become proficient in using these technologies so that they can enhance their productivity and ability to serve the customer efficiently.

Internet

The Internet has become an important part of most consumers' everyday life and its usage grows daily. Any company serving customers must not underestimate its importance. Customers go online to research potential purchases, comparison-shop, get answers to questions, make purchases, check order status, check warranties, and talk to friends and acquaintances on Facebook. The list goes on and on! As customers continue to exercise their desire to use the Internet as a customer service tool, organizations must continuously increase and improve the information and services offered. A company's website can be an important customer service offering. Web addresses on products must be accurate, information on the site must be attractive and up-to-date, and the site must be easy to navigate. An excellent website can actually save a company vital customer service dollars and can complement other technologies offered to the customer. A customer desiring to place an order by phone may hear a message while they are waiting on hold that invites them to place their order over the Internet. At this point, the customer may make a decision to become a coproducer and to look up the Web address. They will likely go online while they are still holding on the phone line. If they can get to the website easily and can see how to place an order, they will likely do so. The customer is served, the order is placed, the customer did not hang up in frustration, and was served in a manner that they hopefully feel great about. In the end the company can count that customer as being served efficiently.

Electronic Mail

Many businesses have incorporated electronic mail programs into their computer systems. Electronic mail, or e-mail, has in many cases eliminated the need for the paper memoranda that clutter employees' mailboxes, desks, and trashcans. It has also shortened the time spent on communications between people and departments. E-mail is probably most beneficial when we are interacting with both internal and external customers. A response that previously would have taken a few days to flow through the company mail system can now be delivered almost immediately. As with other communication technologies in use in customer service, e-mail requires that the user understand how the system works. Numerous companies are sending e-mails to external customers to confirm orders, announce shipping dates, share warranty information, and extend special offers, and the list goes on. One new reality of using e-mail to communicate with customers is that the expected response time has gotten so short that customers may be waiting at their computer for a response. This can sometimes result in unmet expectations on the part of the customer. Therefore, customer service providers must strive for the quickest response time possible.

When using e-mail, users should become familiar with the usage policies of their organizations. There are several practices that are considered appropriate among all e-mail users. The following are some of the most common:

- **Never type in uppercase.** Using capital letters is considered poor etiquette and is harder to read.
- Remember to periodically **clean out your mailbox.** By cleaning out your mailbox, you will be sure to discard old mails and will be reminded of what is current and pending. Check your junk mail periodically. Some e-mail filters may direct important correspondence there incorrectly.
- **Avoid sending personal messages over the system.** When you are communicating electronically, you are usually using someone else's resource. You may also accidentally send your message to the wrong mailbox. Even a secured message can be broken into.
- **Since e-mail has no provision for voice inflection, it is incapable of showing emotion.** Some users like to use *emoticons,* or icons that add emotion to the screen, to add personality to their messages. Books are available that show how to create emoticons.
- Most e-mail can **ask for confirmation that mail has been received.** Use this feature whenever possible.

E-mail has added a new dimension to the challenges of communicating with both internal and external customers. Familiarize yourself with the system in your organization.

Automated Phone Systems

Anyone who has called a 1-800 line has undoubtedly interacted with an automated phone system. Schools, small businesses, and doctor's offices now use some type of automation as a part of their phone system. One huge benefit of an automated phone system is that it replaces the human that used to have to respond to all incoming calls, answer questions, and then connect the caller to the appropriate office. These systems can save payroll dollars and time and can increase efficiency. Unfortunately, the average customer probably has at least one horror story of being caught "in the system."

Companies that use automated phone systems should check the system—essentially call themselves on a regular basis. The volume of the automated speaker or music should be set at a pleasant level. The menu should be accurate and as concise as possible. A system that has a voice recognition feature should actually comprehend the average caller's voice.

All customer service providers should be prompted to pass along any feedback that they receive from customers on problems or potential glitches in the automated system. The use of an automated phone system can be cost effective and an asset if managed properly.

Voice Mail

Most corporations have some type of voice messaging system in place. Customer service providers must be comfortable using their customers' voice mail systems and must understand their own system.

Voice mail systems provide customers and customer service providers with wonderful opportunities for interaction. When customers are not immediately available, messages can be left to provide faster feedback. For customers, **voice mail** systems can allow their calls to be answered faster and the customers know that either the calls will be answered soon or they can leave a recorded message detailing their situation.

When leaving a message on voice mail, practice the following steps to increase customer responsiveness:

1. Speak clearly and slowly; identify yourself, your company, the day and date, and the time.
2. State the reason for your call.
3. Suggest to the customer what the next step should be. Does he or she need to call you back or wait for more information?
4. Leave your name and the phone number where you can be reached. You have already given the customer your name; but, in case he or she did not write it down, give it again with your phone number.
5. Close with a positive farewell.

◀ **voice mail**
A system in which a spoken message is recorded and stored in the recipient's voice mailbox. The recipient can later retrieve the audible message.

Remember that when leaving a recorded message, time may be short, so be as brief and to the point as possible.

Customers may become frustrated with having to talk to "a machine" when they have a question or problem. When answering complaints about voice mail, do not dismiss the complaint as being unimportant. Ask your customer questions so that you can find out what really went wrong. If the customer claims that the system is not working, call it yourself. The best way to find out how well something is working for your customer is to become the customer. If you find that something is malfunctioning in the system or that the system is awkward to work with, share the information with others who can make changes. Sometimes the problem is easily corrected. The music playing in the background may be too loud or may not be tuned in well, an out-of-date holiday greeting may be played, or the voice on the recording may be irritating.

Fax Machines

Fax machines have become necessary fixtures in most offices; but, surprisingly, many people do not know the basic guidelines for using them. When using a fax machine, a fax cover sheet should always be used. A fax cover sheet does not need to be fancy but should include several pieces of key information. Include the following: your name, title, department, company, address, phone number, fax number, number of pages in your fax (including the cover sheet), and an introductory message. If the information you are faxing is confidential, place a warning statement or disclaimer on the cover sheet. The fax cover sheet is the first impression that the recipient has of your company. If your company does not have an official fax cover sheet, create one including all of the pertinent information and possibly your company logo. It will not take long to make it, but the positive impression will be long term.

When faxing information, strive for accuracy. Double-check the number you are calling. A fax will not go through unless you reach another fax machine, and it is unlikely that you would reach another machine if you dialed incorrectly, but it could happen. Make sure that the faxed information is readable. If the print is too small to read easily, enlarge it before faxing. If you have had difficulty in receiving responses after sending a fax, try using a broad-tipped pen and writing ATTENTION or IMPORTANT across the cover sheet.

A faxed signature is in many cases considered as valid as a witnessed signature. This can really shorten the time it takes to do business, but it also places a considerable amount of responsibility on the parties involved.

Whenever possible, fax information after hours. Customers will be pleased because you will not be tying up their machine during peak usage; you will also save on long-distance costs. Finally, make sure that your fax machine is well maintained and that it has an adequate paper supply. A difficult-to-read fax does not speak well of your company.

Texting

An emerging method of communication that businesses are using at an increasing level is texting. Customers' use of their cell phones as their personal "communication central" has gone up dramatically over the last few years. Businesses need to create a method to help customers to communicate in the method that they prefer. This may be by using their cell phone and receiving or sending a text. Numerous businesses have identified effective methods of incorporating texting into their system of doing business. The local pharmacy may send customers a text to indicate that their prescription is ready. A customer may request or confirm an appointment by text. A bank may text customers their available balance on a regular basis. So many new examples have emerged of businesses creatively using this technology. Since not all customers wish to receive texts or may not have affordable texting plans, businesses should never assume that all customers want to communicate in this way. The exciting opportunity that now exists is that it is one more way to serve customers in the manner that they wish to do business.

Developing excellent communication skills can give a customer service provider the best opportunity to communicate with customers in a manner that encourages understanding. The effective incorporation of the five methods of communication—listening, writing, talking, reading, and nonverbal—into our daily lives can provide us with the best means of communicating positively with our customers.

> *"Questions persuade more powerfully than any other form of verbal behavior."*
> **Neil Rackham**

KEY TERMS

communication	nonverbal expression	talking
customer intelligence	pitch	voice inflection
eye contact	reading	voice mail
listening	relationship marketing	writing

QUICK QUIZ

1. Customer service providers must be proficient communicators.   T or F
2. Customer intelligence is the process of gathering information; building a historical database; and developing an understanding of current, potential, and lapsed customers.   T or F
3. Relationship marketing rarely has a positive impact on business.   T or F
4. Identifying why a customer has lapsed can help a business to make a positive change. T or F
5. A good listener plans his or her answer while the speaker is talking.   T or F
6. The way you use your voice does not significantly impact how a message is received.   T or F
7. Taking notes during a phone interaction can be helpful in becoming more organized as you attempt to address customer concerns.   T or F
8. *Can't, never, don't,* and *you have to* would not be considered words to use.   T or F
9. Eye contact can convey sincerity and interest.   T or F
10. E-mail is replacing face-to-face communication with both internal and external customers.   T or F

OPPORTUNITIES FOR CRITICAL THINKING

1. List four words to use and four words to avoid.
2. List and define the five methods of communication.
3. What factors can cause people to have poor listening skills?
4. What characteristics can an individual's voice reveal about him or her?
5. Explore some tactics for recording information received by telephone. What procedures does your company use?
6. How can the development of customer intelligence enhance relationship marketing with specific clients?

7. How should you respond if a face-to-face customer refuses to maintain eye contact?
8. How do you view voice mail systems as a customer? As a customer service provider?
9. What information should be included on a fax cover sheet?
10. Investigate the privacy issues related to e-mail.

SKILL BUILDING

Listening

The need for outstanding listening skills is recognized by most customers and their service providers. One of the biggest obstacles to the development of effective listening skills is a poor self-awareness of our own listening abilities and habits.

Individually or in a group, have someone read the following story aloud. After it has been read, try to answer the accompanying listening comprehension questions from memory. Do not suggest that the listeners take notes, but they may if they initiate it. The reader should read at a normal pace.

Kendall needed to go to the store to pick up a few items for her dinner party. Before she left, she decided to make a shopping list so that she would not forget anything. Unfortunately, she could not locate any paper so she wrote her list on a sack from the 5 & 10 Drug Store. The first item she listed was lettuce, but two heads or one? One would be sufficient. She also needed steaks. Of the eleven people she had invited, only eight had responded to the invitation. Kendall's friends Jacob and Andrew did have a reputation for just showing up, so she determined that she should buy food for two extras.

This meant that she should buy ten steaks. She also needed potatoes, carrots, bread, milk, sour cream, green beans, and two dozen eggs. Kendall considered garnishing her salad with tomatoes but decided against it. She thought that her list was complete but looked in her refrigerator to be sure. One final item that she needed was strawberries for the dessert. Off to the store she went.

Try to answer the following listening comprehension questions, recalling the story that was just read.

1. Who was having the dinner party?
2. How many had confirmed that they were coming to the party?
3. What was on the shopping list?
4. What was the list written on?
5. What type of meat was being served?

Check your answers with the story. If you answered correctly, you are probably a good listener. If you were unable to respond accurately to the questions, you may need to work on improving your listening skills.

Complete the following listening self-assessment to evaluate yourself as a listener.

1. List four of your best qualities as a listener.
2. List four of your most common listening weaknesses (mind wanders, etc.). Rank them from worst to best.
3. How long is your average attention span?
4. List four qualities of outstanding listeners.
5. List any outside distractions that interfere with your ability to be an effective listener.

Examine the answers that you gave to the listening self-assessment questions. Now that you have identified your listening strengths and weaknesses, you can begin to establish an action plan to become a better listener. Write three specific goals that you can work toward to improve your listening and a timetable for the accomplishment of your goals. Outstanding listening skills can be the determining factor between an average customer service provider and an outstanding one. Happy listening!

Ethics in Action

You are the owner of a successful construction company that specializes in custom homes. You have been very busy the last few years. While you are grateful for the success, you no longer can handle every issue for every customer. About 11 months ago you hired a great guy to assist you and work with your customers. You have been very generous with this employee and included him in the company insurance plan, and gave him a company vehicle and considerable flexibility. He is currently working with about eight customers with homes at various degrees of completion and they all love him. To them he is the "face" of the company. Today he very unexpectedly came in and told you that he was going to work for a competitor. He said he appreciated the opportunities that you had given him but that he had to do what was best for his family. He told you that this would be his last day and that he would bring you the keys to his company vehicle as soon as he got his wife's car out of the shop. How do you respond to him? What will you tell the customers that he has been working with?

CHALLENGE   Mystery Shopper

Customer service and satisfaction can be difficult to evaluate. One method of evaluating service levels is through mystery shopping. You may know someone that periodically "shops" a business and then writes an evaluation. If you do an Internet search for mystery shopping, dozens of websites pop up offering employment, sample surveys, and reasons why mystery shopping is important.

Mystery shopping is important because it allows a business or upper management to get a real-life evaluation of how well a business functions when it does not know it is being watched. Most employees can recall a time when "the big boss" was visiting and the employees were instructed to be on their best behavior. While this is a common part of the way that many businesses function, it does not provide a realistic assessment of how customers on a daily basis are treated and how they may perceive the business's service levels.

Challenge Objectives

1. To create a comprehensive questionnaire for observation of customer service.
2. To administer the questionnaire using an observational method.
3. To compile the results of the mystery shopping activity into a usable collection of information.

Assignment

Identify a type of business to evaluate for your mystery shopping activity. Create a comprehensive survey for your use as you "shop" your businesses. Your survey should include at least 10 questions relating to a variety of customer service questions relevant to the industry you are shopping. You may want to refer to the sample question topics for inspiration. Organize your survey in a methodical manner and use a separate form for each business you "shop." These completed surveys will document your results.

Sample Question Topics

Physical appearance of the business
How quickly you were greeted
Ability of customer service representative to answer product questions
Professionalism
Suggestive selling
Pace of the transaction
Detracting factors
Odor
Appearance of employees
Physical layout
Temperature
Parking lot
Adequate lighting
Availability of parking
Feeling of safety
Courtesy of customer service representative
Knowledge of customer service representative
How the customer service representative handled the situation
Overall feeling of satisfaction
Other comments about your customer experience
If you would do business with this company again
If you would recommend this company/product to others
And so on

Presentation

After you have shopped your businesses, review the results. Prepare a fact sheet for each business evaluated. Your fact sheet should provide clear information and any pertinent details that further explain the responses.

Fact sheets should be typed, well organized, and professionally written. Remember, mystery shopping is a tool so that a business can have another set of eyes and experiences. The goal is to have a better understanding of how the business is really serving its customers.

You may find that you enjoy being a mystery shopper and want to consider it as a possible career opportunity!

ANSWERS TO QUICK QUIZ

1. T	5. F	9. T
2. T	6. F	10. T
3. F	7. T	
4. T	8. T	

Coping with Challenging Customers

Remember This

Nothing gives one person so much advantage as to remain cool and unruffled under all circumstances.

Thomas Jefferson

CHAPTER OBJECTIVES

In this chapter, you will learn how to

- List reasons that customers are challenging.
- Explain the five tips to keep from creating challenging customers.
- Explain the productive nature of empathy.
- Define responsibility check.
- Discuss what to do when you make mistakes with customers.

From Chapter 7 of *Customer Service: A Practical Approach*. Sixth Edition. Elaine K. Harris. Copyright © 2013 by Pearson Education, Inc. All rights reserved.

Who Are Challenging Customers?

As we interact with others in our daily lives, we become painfully aware of the fact that some individuals are easier and more enjoyable to be around and to spend time with than others. Those individuals who, for one reason or another, "bother" us are the people that we probably attempt to avoid. Unfortunately, in business, we cannot avoid our customers. In fact, we are frequently required to spend the greatest amount of our time with those customers that we find the most challenging.

challenging customers Those customers with problems, questions, fears, and personalities that require us to work to achieve true communication.

Who are challenging customers? **Challenging customers** are those customers with problems, questions, fears, and personalities that require us to work to achieve true communication. Because all individuals have their own unique personalities and sets of past experiences, individuals will not find the same customers challenging. Although challenging customers may be difficult to interact with, the reality is that they are still our customers and our overall goal is to provide them with excellent customer service and a feeling of satisfaction with their experience.

Why Are Customers Challenging?

Customers may be seen as challenging for a wide variety of reasons. They may have personalities or communication styles that we find difficult to interact with. Thus, customers may be seen as challenging without having done anything specific to us. Customers may be perceived as challenging because of any or all of the following reasons:

- They do not speak your language.
- They do not have expertise or an understanding of the specific product or situation.
- They may be openly hostile.
- They are visibly upset about something (and it may not have anything to do with you or your company).
- They are very quiet and noncommunicative.
- They show an attitude of superiority.
- They are impatient.
- They imply that they are doing you and your company a big favor for doing business with you.
- They appear to embody the type of person that you have a personal bias against.
- They are so nice that you hate to have to give them bad news.
- They are extremely angry.
- They have difficulty in making decisions.

Everyone is someone's challenging customer. Customers want to believe that they are the most important persons in our lives at this moment.

As we strive to provide excellent customer service, each customer should be the most important person at the moment. Challenging customers are never challenging by accident. They come into our interactions with past experiences, perceptions, expectations, frustrations, the stresses of daily life, and the desire for us to show that we value them as our customers. Customer service providers also bring their own unique sets of ideas to an interaction. The difference between the two is that the customer service provider is responsible for building the bridge of communication.

"The best bridge between despair and hope is a good night's sleep."
E. Joseph Cossman

Are You Creating Challenging Customers?

Some customers are just challenging, no matter what we do or do not do for them. Most individuals who work with the public believe that they do a good job of interacting with their customers, but the reality is that at times we may create many of the customer problems that we experience. While we should be thankful for the customers who are for the most part happy and cooperative, our mannerisms or comments may "rub them the wrong way" or really offend them and cause them to become irritable or uncooperative.

Five Tips to Keep from Creating Challenging Customers

1. **Respect the customer's time:** Always work at peak efficiency. It is easy to fall into a laid-back manner of dealing with those that we feel comfortable with. Stay focused on the customer.
2. **Do not impose your bad or negative mood on anyone else:** Everyone has a bad day once in a while, but customers should never be able to tell that you are having a rough day. Both customers and customer service providers have problems, but customers do not enter into the customer experience to hear what is going on in your life. People will avoid dealing with you if you earn the reputation of being moody or having up and down days. Do not neglect your interactions with your internal customers. It is not enough to be nice to your external customers and then to treat your coworkers negatively. Frequently, if you immerse yourself in doing your job and being positive, you will forget what was bothering you and will have a better day than you expected.
3. **Recognize regular customers with a smile and try to learn their names:** Customers must value the experience they have by doing business with your organization. It is not too much for them to expect that you would remember them from one interaction to another. Giving someone a look of recognition is a great place to start. Recognizing customers starts with deciding that you are going to make the effort to do it. Everyone feels more welcome and a part of things if they think

that someone else recognizes them. Try for one week to call everyone possible by name, including your internal customers, and you will see positive results. You may increase the morale in your work area and you will end your workday feeling like you have a lot of new friends! People usually choose to do business with people they like!

4. **Avoid destructive remarks:** Insults or little "zingers" that seem like creative and "smart" responses may seem appropriate and may give you the satisfaction of having the last word and make you feel like the winner now. In the long run, they will make you the big loser. Some customers may seek ways to get back at you, and others may avoid you and your company because they were hurt or assume that the entire organization is as rude as you were. The Golden Rule is a good one to follow in this situation. If you would not want someone to say it to you, do not say it to them. In the long run, destructive remarks are just that, destructive.

5. **Show initiative:** Show customers that you are willing to complete a task or go the extra mile for them. Laziness abounds in our society today. What a refreshing experience to do business with someone who offers to do a little something extra or to carry through a project to the end. Customers may not expect to work with someone with initiative, so you will be a hero in their eyes.

Characteristics of Challenging Customers

Challenging customers can be categorized in many different ways. The following are 10 characteristics of challenging customers. Remember, challenging customers are frequently challenging because of who we are, not who they are.

TEAM TIME

Sit down with your team and discuss the question, "Are you creating challenging customers?" Attempt to be honest in your assessment. Most organizations have challenging customers; the difficulty is identifying whether or not you are creating them. Refer to the *five tips to keep from* *creating challenging customers* as you conduct your discussion. If your team determines that you may be creating challenging customers, develop an action plan to stop doing so. Sometimes the easiest way to stop having to deal with challenging customers is to stop creating them!

1. Language and/or cultural barriers: As our society continues to include people from other cultures, we will increasingly come into contact with individuals who speak English as a second language or who barely speak English at all. Communication can be challenging, even when we speak the same language. When attempting to communicate with others who have difficulty with English, speak slowly and clearly. Avoid using slang terms that are hard to translate. If words are not conveying the intended message, try illustrating with hand motions. Do not pretend that you understand what the customer said if that is not the case. Ask questions and repeat what you understood. Try not to become frustrated. Even customers who have a hard time understanding our spoken messages deserve patience. They are still our customers. Sometimes, writing out the message makes it easier for non-English-speaking persons to understand, because they can refer to their dictionaries. Keep an appropriate language dictionary handy so that you can clarify what they are saying.

If all else fails, suggest that the customer call back or come back with an English-speaking friend who can help resolve his or her situation. Identify the most common languages that are dealt with in your business in your part of the country. The languages that these customers speak may be appropriate languages for you to begin to learn. Many customer service-oriented companies are requiring fluency in specific languages as a condition for employment.

Some individuals offend those from other cultures out of ignorance. Learn about the cultures of your customers. Information is readily available, and all will benefit from the insights into customers' native traditions, ways of doing business, concerns, and beliefs. America is a melting pot of unique individuals with something to offer and with dollars to spend with either your organization or someone else's.

2. Older customers: American society is getting older. As this fact becomes more and more apparent, it becomes important to recognize the characteristics of older customers. First of all, what does it mean to be older? Different people will give different responses. For our purposes, older customers will be defined as those customers who are 65 years of age and older. This is a significant percentage of the American population. The stereotypes of an older person as one who is incapable of making decisions and having little discretionary income are ideas of the past. Today's 65+ customer is independent, active, self-sufficient, and living life to the fullest.

When dealing with older customers, customer service providers must remember to treat them with respect and attention. Their purchasing power is extremely significant. Older customers may require some special attention. They may have some trouble reading fine print, may have a slightly slower response time, or may be slightly hard of hearing. When interacting with an older person, always show a high level of respect. Recognize the individual's need for self-respect. While many older customers are pleased to find out that they are eligible for senior citizen discounts, some may not appreciate being informed that they qualify. Never talk down to an older person by referring to them as "little lady" or "young man." Although you may be trying to warm up to them, such expressions just call more attention to them.

If you notice that customers are having difficulty in reading, suggest that they move to a better-lit area; if they are still having difficulty, offer to read the information to them. Many older people have trouble hearing. A simple approach for helping them to understand what you are saying is to look at them while you are talking so that they can see your lips moving. Do not shout, as this draws undue attention. Do speak clearly, at a moderate pace, and do not mumble.

Older customers may be unfamiliar with some current technology. This is certainly not necessarily the case, but it may be. If customers are not currently in the workforce and do not work with items such as computers, fax machines, the Internet, and cash registers, they may find them overwhelming. On the other hand, some older customers may be much more proficient than we are because they have invested time in learning new technologies. If customers seem to be unsure of how to use equipment, ask if you may be of assistance. If they accept your offer, assist them in a positive manner. If they refuse your offer, allow them to figure it out for themselves.

3. Impatient customers: People today operate at a fast pace. As we go about our daily personal and business lives, we are often attempting to accomplish many tasks within a short time. Often the challenge is not attainable. Our customers are attempting to do the same thing. The rush to fit everything in can cause customers to become impatient. When customers are impatient or irritable, it is important to remember that they may be bothered by something beyond our control—a traffic snarl, a headache, or a dread of completing the task at hand. There are times when their impatience is due to something that we have done or due to an antiquated system of doing business.

When calling customers on the telephone, always ask if you are calling at a convenient time. A customer who is in the middle of doing something important is likely to express his or her impatience to us and may be distracted as we talk. Emphasize to your customers that your goal is to work with them as efficiently as possible. Tell them that you have their interests in mind. Stay on the task at hand and complete their business quickly and accurately. Impatient customers may complain that you are disrupting their work or are bothering them. Strive to show the impatient customers, through your actions, that your company is worth the investment of their time.

4. Angry customers: Unfortunately, anger is a common emotion in customer service. Both internal and external customers experience anger from time to time. Anger among internal customers, if improperly managed, can create an all-out war between departments—a situation that does not promote easy internal customer service in the future.

Many external customers call with customer service challenges only when they are angry. Anger can be like a dynamite waiting to explode. If not properly defused, it can cause quite a commotion.

To respond to a customer's anger, try to calm the customer. It is important for the customer service provider to stay calm. Angry customers have the ability to bring out anger in everyone with whom they come into contact. Ask the customer to explain his or her situation. Allow customers to vent their situation and feelings. They will feel better when they get it all out. Do not interrupt them; let them get it out, and then respond. Acknowledge the customer's emotions, but find out the facts. As the customer is explaining, he or she may be losing some of the original fury. The customer has found someone who is willing to listen. Attempt to find effective solutions to the situation.

Angry people can become abusive or may resort to the use of profanity. This puts the customer service provider in a difficult situation. Should he or she take the abuse or stop it and risk making the customer even more angry? One response to a customer's use of vulgar language is to say, "I realize that you are upset, but I am not used to being spoken to in this way; please limit your explanation to the facts." Always approach customers with respect, even when they are behaving in an unprofessional manner. Acknowledge their emotions; but, as quickly as possible, look for an opening to gain control of the conversation. Phrases like "I recognize your frustration…" or "Let's find a positive conclusion to this situation" are lead-in sentences that may allow the customer service provider to take charge. Customer anger provides the opportunity for a new relationship to begin and can have a positive result.

5. Analytical customers: Customers who are analytical tend to need facts and like to know that they are speaking with someone who is knowledgeable about his or her product or company. They frequently take an objective approach to decision making and problem solving. Analytical people rarely show their emotions and are not concerned about your emotions. They are not concerned with whether or not you like them.

Analytical customers like consistency and proof. When dealing with customers who want facts and definite answers, treat them with respect and give them what they want. Tell them how a bill was figured, what the billing dates are, when the interest rate is going up, and anything else that they ask that you can give a factual response to. Ask them if they have additional questions, and answer them efficiently.

6. Noncommittal customers: Some customers have difficulty in making decisions. They may be unwilling to commit because they are seeking information from several sources, or they may be hesitant in making a decision. Individuals seem noncommittal for a variety of reasons. They may have been too quick in the past to commit to one option and then have regretted their choice. They may have financial constraints that require them to carefully survey all options and determine the short-term and long-term feasibility of a decision. Other customers may have to consider the expectations of their superiors or coworkers who are not present but who will also benefit from the decision.

When interacting with noncommittal customers, keep in mind that customers are not slow to decide because they want to frustrate you. They have their own reasons for being hesitant to commit. To help them to a speedier decision, detail the possible options. Ask if there is anything that you have not explained. Suggest that they make a decision today. If they are not ready to do this, suggest a timetable that would allow a moderate amount of time for their consideration of a decision. The timetable will give them a deadline to work toward and will diminish the possibility that the information that you have shared with them will become out of date.

7. Superior customers: Some customers may present to the customer service provider the impression that they are in some way superior. It is important not to take this type of attitude seriously. Customers who show an attitude of superiority can be frustrating to interact with. They may be rude or may make condescending remarks. In reality, customers who present themselves in this manner are frequently very insecure and feel as though they can somehow seem better if they put someone else down. They want you to know how important they consider themselves.

When dealing with this type of customer, the customer service provider must recognize his or her own self-worth. The temptation is strong to enter into a competition with the customer to see who really is better, but this is an unproductive waste of time, and no one really wins in the end. When possible, use the customer's attitude of superiority to your advantage. Praise his or her accomplishments and importance. Suggest that your resolution of their situations will enhance their customer's position. By helping the customer to see that he or she will be the winner in the end, the competition can be reduced.

8. Immature customers: It is probable that a customer service provider will have the opportunity to interact with many immature customers. A great deal of customer service centers around problem solving, and immature customers are likely to have some problems. Late or unpaid bills, excuses, or blaming others for their problems are common occurrences among immature customers. When interacting with immature customers, listen to their explanation of the situation before responding. Allow them to fully describe their problem or question. When responding, be frank about the consequences that may result from not paying bills and other similar dilemmas. If they have questions, answer them fully. Your perception may be that they are asking something that "everyone knows," but they apparently do not if they are asking. Immature customers need to know that their actions affect others. Stress the importance of your company policies and the need to treat all customers fairly and consistently.

Immature customers may really not know any better than to act and react in the manner that they are sharing with you. Customers who complain about having to pay a large utility bill on time and say that if they pay it, they will not have any money left to go out to eat probably need a "reality check." Be firm with them. They may not appreciate your enforcing your company's policies now, but in the future they will learn from the experience.

9. Talkative customers: Talkative customers can be exciting to be around. They may be outgoing and may have interesting stories to tell. They are often good storytellers and may secretly enjoy hearing themselves talk. Although we may periodically enjoy being around talkative people, we must still conduct business efficiently. Some talkative customers may be difficult to be around.

When communicating with talkative customers, approach them in a positive and open manner. Allow them to share their questions or concerns. Help them to stay on the subject by asking specific questions that further explain the situation. Express your interest in rectifying their circumstances. Show appreciation for their knowledge and abilities. Operate at a fast pace, use humor to keep the discussion focused, and ask them if they have further questions. Conclude by expressing appreciation for their patience and understanding. It is sometimes hard to terminate conversations with talkative customers; try a phrase that suggests that they are on a time schedule. "I don't want to take any more of your limited time" may be an effective closing.

10. Customers with special needs: Customer service providers may from time to time have customers who require additional assistance because of a special need. Special needs customers include all customers who, because of individual circumstances, require our productive cooperation. It may be difficult to recognize a special needs customer, because many individuals who are viewed by society as having special needs do not perceive themselves in this way.

When communicating with someone with a disability, consider the following:

- If a person has a hearing loss, speak directly to the person. If they have an interpreter or assistant with them, acknowledge them but continue to speak to the customer. Speak clearly and slowly, facing the individual. Include appropriate facial expressions since people who are deaf depend a lot on facial expressions and gestures for communication cues.
- If a person is in a wheelchair, try to communicate with them at eye level. Do not touch the wheel chair or any walking appliance. This would be considered a violation of their personal space.
- If a person is visually impaired, never play with or talk to a guide dog; you will distract the animal from its job.
- If a person has a speech impediment, be patient and listen carefully. Avoid the temptation to finish their sentences for them.

Additionally, you should never assume someone needs or wants help—but do not be afraid to inquire politely. For example, simply say, "May I be of assistance?"

As always, special needs customers should be treated with respect. Strive to understand their questions and concerns, and attempt to provide appropriate solutions.

Respect: A Classic Idea that Still Works!

As our society becomes more focused on the unique differences among individuals of different ages, it is easy to fall into the "generation gap syndrome." This is the idea that individuals who grew up at different times and shared different life-shaping experiences cannot ever really communicate. This could not be a more incorrect notion! People of all ages can communicate and coexist peacefully, but the necessary ingredient is respect. **Respect** means to give someone recognition or special regard.

respect To give someone recognition or special regard.

To respect or to show respect for someone else does not minimize our own self-worth. Instead it allows the opportunity for us to learn from someone else and to grow in ways that we would not if we interacted only with those just like us. Respect is not limited to those in a different age group but should be shown to all others. By using courtesy titles like "Sir," "Ma'am," "Mr.," and "Mrs.," we show professionalism and demonstrate the regard we have for the other individual as our customer. If a customer does not desire to be addressed this formally, we should follow through with his or her wishes. Never show condescension. Talking down to customers, even *very* young ones, only makes them feel uncomfortable and may make them angry. There is also the implication that customers are unable to understand the information that we are sharing with them. Finally, show respect for customers' knowledge. Customers today are better informed and more sophisticated than they ever have been in history. Age, sex, race, education, and so on have no real bearing on what a customer may have an in-depth knowledge of. If we allow ourselves to recognize the knowledge of our customers, we will benefit and end up learning from them.

Job Link

Think about the customer group that you find to be the most challenging. Try to identify why that group is challenging to you. List five things that you can do to better serve that customer group. Post the list in your work area and the next time you encounter your own most challenging customer give it a try. Both you and your customer will benefit!

Understanding the Positive Power of Empathy

Empathy is the ability to understand what someone is experiencing and to take action to assist in resolving the situation. Empathy is productive. When we show people empathy, we do not express our sorrow over their situation. Instead we listen to their explanation of the situation and say, "What can we do to help you?" The main focus of empathy is problem solving.

If a customer calls to say that he or she is late paying a bill because there was a death in the immediate family, he or she has obviously suffered an emotional experience. By showing empathy, we convey that we are sorry to hear of the loss and would like to minimize stress if we can. Perhaps we can arrange an extended due date for the billing or arrange for special financing. In either case, the customer service provider is helping the customer to resolve his or her problems rather than dwelling on them.

empathy The ability to understand what someone is experiencing and to take action to assist in resolving the situation.

Responsibility Check

Businesses walk a fine line with regard to customer service. In most cases, a business has what the customer wants and needs, but a business must be managed with profitability in mind. Sometimes a customer will make an unjustified request for service. This request may put the customer service provider and the business where he or she works in an awkward position. Should the customer service provider provide the service and risk profitability or refuse to provide the service and risk losing a customer?

One method for dealing with this type of situation is to perform a responsibility check. A **responsibility check** is assessing a situation and determining who *should* have responsibility and who really *does* have the responsibility. Sometimes a customer is unhappy with us for not doing something that was really his or her responsibility. To provide excellent customer service, the customer must be permitted to participate in the process and not just benefit from it. Accountabilities must be created and enforced.

responsibility check Assessing a situation and determining who *should* have responsibility and who really *does* have the responsibility.

An example is a situation in which a responsibility check is appropriate between a student and a professor. In an educational setting, the students are the customers and the professor is the customer service provider. The overall goal is to provide the student with the opportunity for learning with the positive outcome of a good grade. The professor needs to keep his or her students satisfied so that they will continue to enroll in classes, but at the same time he or she must strive to maintain the integrity of the course and institution for all students. If a student/customer who has not attended class and who is not succeeding approaches his or her professor and suggests that since the student is the customer the student should receive a good grade for the class, the professor must perform a responsibility check. Whose responsibility is it to enable the student to earn a good grade? It is a joint responsibility between the professor and student. The professor must provide pertinent information, be available to answer questions, and test fairly. The student must attend class, read the textbook, and study. The student was not living up to his or her responsibility. If the student is not making the necessary contribution, it would detract from the integrity of the course if the professor gave the student a better grade. When providing customer service, all customers must be considered, not just a few.

The goal in performing a responsibility check is to clarify what went wrong in a situation and to shift the responsibility to the responsible party. The shifting of responsibility can be enhanced by coproduction of customer service. A responsibility check is a positive approach to creating the opportunity for excellent customer service by requiring all who are involved to participate in the process and to take responsibility. A responsibility check must be handled tactfully, but it can create an opportunity for better customer service to all customers.

"The journey toward excellence is a never-ending road."
H. James Harrington

What to Do When You Are Wrong

As a customer service provider interacts with his or her customers, the possibility exists that he or she will not treat all customers as well as they should be treated. Customer service providers are only human and may be tempted to take out their frustrations on their customers, or they may make mistakes. When you believe that you have treated a customer inappropriately, try the following:

- **Review the situation:** Examine your behavior and the words that have been spoken. Try to look at the situation from the customer's point of view.
- **Observe the customer's reaction:** Is the customer visibly upset? Does the customer seem surprised or hurt by your actions?
- **Admit the mistake:** Whether or not it was an error in your information or judgment, it is always best to acknowledge that you are aware of it.
- **Apologize for your actions or error:** Express to the customer that you regret the problem, but do not make excuses for why it occurred.
- **Find a solution and implement it:** The most effective way to undo the improper treatment of a customer is to create an effective solution and to put it into effect as quickly as possible.

Six Super Ways to Cope with Challenging Customers

1. **Listen:** Allow customers to express their concern or to share their side of the story.
2. **Ask questions:** Seek clarification of the problem. Determine the variables involved.

3. **Show empathy:** Attempt to understand what the customer is experiencing and take action to assist in resolving the situation.
4. **Solve the problem:** Determine the most appropriate solution to the situation. Use creativity and follow company policies as you seek to create a positive outcome for both the customer and your organization.
5. **Follow up:** Restate what has been decided and how the situation is being resolved. Ask the customer if he or she has any more questions.
6. **End on a positive note:** Thank customers for their understanding. Bid them farewell in an enthusiastic manner so that they remember the professional manner in which you resolved their problem. Customers are more likely to remember the end of an interaction than the beginning.

⬤ Payoffs of Coping with Challenging Customers

Customer service providers must think of their customers as long-term assets! Keeping in mind that it is much easier to retain an established customer than it is to recruit new customers, the customer service provider should be extremely motivated to resolve challenging customers' problems. Customers should be made to feel better at the end of an interaction than they felt at the beginning. It is easy to take care of customers when things are going well; it is when things become challenging that difficulties may arise.

We learn to deal with conflict by confronting it. When we require ourselves to develop skills or to learn new information, we are creating an environment where we can become better at managing conflict. Challenging people are a reality of customer service! Knowing how to handle them appropriately can reduce both our customers' stress and our own. By learning to cope with challenging customers, we become more effective and efficient assets to our company and the job that we were hired to perform.

KEY TERMS

challenging customers	respect
empathy	responsibility check

QUICK QUIZ

1. Avoidance is an excellent technique for managing challenging customers. T or F
2. Everyone is someone's challenging customer. T or F
3. Respecting the customer's time is one way to keep from creating challenging customers. T or F
4. Using insults or little "zingers" shows how creative and smart you are. T or F

5. A customer service provider should emphasize to his or her customers that his or her goal is to work with them as efficiently as possible.   T or F

6. Respect is the ability to understand what someone is experiencing and to take action to assist in resolving the situation.   T or F

7. A responsibility check is assessing a situation and determining who should have responsibility and who really does have the responsibility.   T or F

8. Customer service providers should never admit that they were wrong.   T or F

9. Showing empathy is highly unprofessional.   T or F

10. There are few measurable benefits of coping with challenging customers.   T or F

OPPORTUNITIES FOR CRITICAL THINKING

1. Explain *responsibility check.*
2. Why are some customers challenging to one individual and not to another?
3. List and explain five characteristics of challenging customers.
4. What type of customer do you find to be the most challenging and why?
5. What are some methods of response to an angry customer who becomes verbally abusive?
6. How can you end discussions with overly talkative customers without offending them?
7. Contrast empathy and sympathy. Which is more productive?
8. Share a situation in which you gave a customer incorrect information and then corrected your mistake.
9. Why is it important to end every customer interaction on a positive note?
10. What are some of the payoffs of coping with challenging customers?

SKILL BUILDING

Coping with Challenging Customers

Customers may be challenging for a variety of reasons. In some instances, customers are not doing anything to challenge us other than just being themselves. Challenging customers are a reality of professional life, especially in the customer service industry.

One of the best methods of becoming more comfortable with challenging customers is to practice. Resolve the following "What would you do?" scenarios.

◼ In your job as a receptionist in the international affairs department, you have the opportunity to interact with numerous people each week. Even though you consider yourself to be a good communicator, you sometimes feel frustrated as you attempt to communicate with some of your non-English-speaking customers. What can you do to improve your skills in communicating with these challenging customers?

◼ You work in the order confirmation department of a large catalog company. Part of your job responsibility is to call suppliers to confirm the ship dates for ordered goods. You spend your entire day on the telephone and for the most part enjoy your job. Your only real frustration is that when you call a few of your customers they react impatiently and rush to get off of the phone. What can you do to improve your skills in communicating with impatient customers?

◀ In your position of residential services coordinator at a major telephone company, you encounter customer problems and concerns daily. While most customers state their situation and are open to your information and knowledge, you do have one type of customer that you find to be challenging. Today, you had a call from a customer angry about receiving a cancellation notice from your company due to nonpayment on the account. As you discuss the situation, the customer tells you that she thinks that it is unfair to expect a payment every month and that your rates are too high. She goes on to tell you that if she paid her bill in full and on time, she would not have any money left over to eat out. You recognize that this customer is lacking maturity; how do you respond appropriately to this and similar customers?

Ethics in Action

You have just made an informational presentation to a group of enrollees in your new benefits program. You represent the insurance company and will only be at this location for two days. One of the enrollees approaches you and starts to critique your presentation. You aren't sure how to react. As you are formulating a response, he starts to cry. What do you do?

CHALLENGE Quality Recognition Form

A unique way to encourage employees to recognize coworkers for going above and beyond is the use of Quality Recognition Forms. Quality Recognition Forms may be known by different names, but their purpose is to create a culture where expressing appreciation and publicly noting someone else's contribution are encouraged. Companies are using this idea in a variety of different ways. In some cases, the forms are available within a company's internal network. In these instances, the form can be completed on the employee's desktop computer and then submitted. Sometimes the submission of the form is to a supervisory or management person and then to the employee being recognized. In other cases, it may just go to the supervisor and into the employee's file. The same type of submission can occur with just a paper copy. The use of this type of recognition can also be used as a means for employees to receive awards (monetary, time off, extra long lunch, qualifying for a raise, etc.).

One of the most important aspects of this type of recognition program is that it gets away from the usual way of doing business. Contrary to a traditional recognition system in which excellence is identified from the top down, it allows employees to cheer each other on. This creates a culture in which employees want to highlight their coworkers' successes. This tends to be a culture that a success-oriented customer service professional wants to work in.

Challenge Objectives

1. To identify the criteria necessary to be recognized for excellence in quality.
2. To demonstrate the initiative necessary to complete and communicate, in writing, an observance of quality.
3. To observe the positive result that can come from recognizing and celebrating someone else's good work.

Assignment

Create a list of criteria that you believe are important to identifying excellence in quality. They can be as broad or as specific as you like. If possible, use your current workplace as your source for evaluation. Your criteria list should have a minimum of five components; as many as ten are appropriate. Complete more than one draft of your criteria and edit it so that you express yourself in the most professional manner possible.

Presentation

Remove or make a copy of the Quality Recognition Form. Complete the form in full. Attempt to be as clear as possible as you explain the quality performance that you have observed. You may want to create a rough draft of your description and proofread it so that your final description is as professional as possible. When you submit your completed form, attach to it the criteria list that you created and used to identify excellence in quality.

◖ **Helpful Hint:** The Quality Recognition Form (the form could be renamed) is an excellent motivation/recognition tool. Think about proposing this to your own employer or company. Some companies use this within the company, sometimes delivered online, as a way for employees at all levels to recognize outstanding performances from their coworkers. Share the idea with your supervisor. It may be your way to be recognized as the professional that you are working to become!

ANSWERS TO QUICK QUIZ

1. F
2. T
3. T
4. F

5. T
6. F
7. T
8. F

9. F
10. F

Quality Recognition Form

(Please provide enough detail for proper evaluation)

I recognize _____ for the quality achievement of

_____

_____

_____

_____

_____

_____

_____

_____

_____

Signed _____

Dated _____

(please circle one)
- Individual
- Team/Group (list team members)

Motivation

Motivation

Remember This

The reward of a job well done is to have done it.

Ralph Waldo Emerson

CHAPTER OBJECTIVES

In this chapter, you will learn how to

- Define motivation.
- Differentiate between needs and wants.
- List common motivating factors.
- Explain the impact that high or low morale may have on an organization.

- Perform your own self-assessment identifying individual strengths and weaknesses.
- Share your own methods of self-motivation with others.

What Is Motivation?

Every professional is at one time or another faced with the challenge of finding the motivation to perform a task or to fulfill an obligation. **Motivation** is the individual drive that causes us to behave in a particular way. Motivation is very personal. Different people are motivated by different rewards, experiences, and circumstances. The motivating force that causes one individual to get up every morning would not necessarily be enough to get his or her next-door neighbor out of bed. It is because of the personal nature of motivation that managers, coworkers, and individuals are continuously seeking to develop a better understanding of what is necessary to create motivation. Motivation is important in both our personal and professional lives. Motivation may be the push that gets us started or the gasoline that keeps us going.

motivation The individual drive that causes us to behave in a particular way.

Employees who work together will have differing levels of motivation at any given time. This suggests that coworkers will not be involved in the same set of circumstances and may have more or less desire to accomplish a task or to work more quickly. An employee who will be starting a week's vacation as soon as his or her work is completed may be especially motivated to complete the work. His or her coworkers who do not have a vacation to look forward to may be less motivated to work hard. When motivation levels vary, it is helpful to work within a group. In this instance, the possibility exists that when one employee is less motivated, others will be more motivated. Unfortunately, this is frequently not the case. One or more of the employees may perform the bulk of the work while the others reap the benefits. This circumstance can greatly reduce motivation over time.

Motivation in customer service should ideally come from management to employee. Several methods of encouragement can be implemented to keep the enthusiasm of customer service providers high. Recognition programs, suggestion rewards, and daily encouragement all help to keep customer service providers feeling good about the roles they are playing in the overall provision of excellent customer service.

Some organizations create unique strategies to motivate their employees. Humor has been found to be an important part of today's motivated workplace. Individual companies approach the use of humor in different ways, but in most instances it can lighten a possibly stressful environment. Studies have shown that laughter can be the key to increased morale and overall job satisfaction. Humorous job titles, jokes of the day that come up on screen when the computer is turned on, and theme dress days can all add humor to the professional workplace.

Other companies offer their employees the opportunity to participate in snack days when all employees bring their favorite "munchies," casual dress days, the opportunity to participate on the company softball team or to sit in company seats at a basketball game or symphony concert, annual company activities, monthly birthday celebrations, and numerous other creative motivational activities. The motivating force behind these activities is that they enhance the unity of the employees. They create shared experiences that can bond employees to each other. Employees who see themselves as an important part of a team are likely to feel a stronger sense of motivation.

Unfortunately, this type of positive leadership is not always available. In those situations, customer service providers must take responsibility for their own motivation.

◖ Needs and Wants

needs Our personal requirements.

When attempting to understand the diversities of motivation, it is helpful to define *needs* and *wants*. **Needs** are our personal requirements. Some needs are instinctive, or primary, like the need for air and food. Other needs are learned, like the specific foods that we enjoy or do not care for; these needs are called secondary needs. Both primary and secondary needs are vital to motivation. Many individuals have difficulty in viewing their real needs and may confuse them with wants. For example, most adults need some form of transportation to enable them to get to work and to fulfill their obligations. They *need* a basic automobile or access to public transportation, but in response to their needs they may *want* a sleek new car.

wants Things or experiences that are desired.

Wants are things or experiences that are desired. Wants have little relationship to needs. While the satisfaction of our needs satisfies our personal requirements, wants have little or nothing to do with what we must have. Individuals commonly desire what they do not really need. While this fact helps to drive the American economy, it may set some individuals up for disappointment if they are unable to obtain what they perceive as their needs. Needs and wants are extremely motivational. Most individuals are willing to work hard to get what they want or need. Wants may be related to our self-image and reflect a desire to display to others our success or perceived success. A salesperson who is having difficulty in making his or her commission may, upon receiving a large check, purchase a prestige watch. In this instance, the salesperson's need to show himself or herself and others that he or she is successful may overshadow the need to pay rent.

"There's only one corner of the universe you can be certain of improving and that is yourself."
Aldous Huxley

When applying an understanding of needs and wants to motivation in a professional environment, misconceptions are common. What management may perceive as being the needs of its employees may in reality have little importance and may result in having little motivational effect. An employee who has a day off coming but must work overtime so that he or she can take it may obtain little or no motivational value from the day off. As frequently happens when attempting to understand expectations and perceptions, incorrect analysis may be made.

Motivating Factors

People have been trying to understand motivation for many years. Numerous studies have been conducted in the attempt to fully understand what motivates individuals. Motivation can be both positive and negative. A positive motivation would drive a travel agent to book enough vacations so that he or she would qualify for a free trip. A negative motivation may drive people focused on losing weight to starve themselves. In both cases, motivation exists. It appears that the motivation to win the trip is of a more positive nature.

Some common motivating factors that have been discovered among adults are

- Individual respect
- Challenging work
- Encouragement from management
- Financial security
- Opportunities to express creativity
- Job security
- Opportunities for advancement
- Unified work environment
- Good benefits
- A project approaching completion
- An approaching vacation
- Recognition from others
- Positive relationship with customers

While all adults may not be motivated by all of the preceding circumstances, many will find them to be driving forces that help them to stay focused and to accomplish their goals. Individuals must become familiar with their individual motivating factors. Frequently, employers fail to recognize the diversity of the factors that may motivate their employees. Instead, they may focus too much attention on the motivation realized from the employees' paycheck. When the company is unable to increase the employees' pay level, the employer may perceive that the motivation is gone. Studies have shown that many adults believe that as long as their basic needs are being covered by their incomes, they will realize more motivation from other factors than just their paychecks.

Recognition is another motivating factor that may be misunderstood. A manufacturing company developed a program of recognizing outstanding employees by honoring them with a special luncheon and a commemorative mug. While the employees were honored to receive the special recognition, they were disappointed to find that the company made no special announcements to the other employees that the special employees had been honored. The only way for the honored employees' peers to hear about the honor was for the outstanding employees to spread the word themselves. This diminished the motivation that resulted from the honor.

Understanding of Morale

◀ **morale** An individual's or group's feelings or attitudes toward a job, supervisor, or company.

Morale is an individual's or group's feelings or attitudes toward a job, supervisor, or company. High morale may result when employees are feeling good about their work, a high level of overall satisfaction is occurring, and employees are secure in their jobs. During high morale, employee loyalty and dedication are strong. High morale may be created by supportive management; a unified work environment; and individual, department, or corporate successes. High morale may result in increased productivity. Because employees are feeling good about their situation, they are less likely to miss work and are more likely to make an appropriate contribution while they are there.

Low morale is when employees and, possibly, management are feeling less positive about their work and organization. Low morale may be caused by poor management, negative employees sharing their dissatisfaction with others, a company's uncertain future, rumored layoffs, too much work or overtime, and smaller-than-expected salary increases. Low morale can result in absenteeism, unprofessional behavior, and high turnover. Low morale may be difficult to correct. Even managers who are aware that it exists may have difficulty in changing it.

A company that announces on the television news that it will be laying off a number of its employees within the next several months will probably see a decline in the morale of its employees. If employees are uncertain of their employment future, they may find it difficult to have a positive feeling toward their organization and everyone associated with it.

TEAM TIME

Sit down with your team and discuss the concept of morale. Remember, *morale is an individual's or group's feelings or attitudes toward a job, supervisor, or company.* Try to identify what the morale level is in your department and company. If morale is high, determine what has contributed to the high level of overall satisfaction with the company. If morale is low, consider what has caused this to happen.

Whether morale is high or low, create a list of the factors that have caused morale to be at that level. Discuss with your team your findings. If morale is low, consider what your team could do to raise morale.

If you are fortunate enough to work for a company or department that has high morale, congratulations! Although morale is not the only determining factor of happiness in the workplace, it is an important one to pay attention to.

◖ Self–Concept and Motivation

Self-concept and motivation are linked in the process of enabling individuals to work productively with others. **Self-concept** is the way in which a person sees himself or herself and thinks that others see him or her. An individual with a strong self-concept is able to view his or her own abilities in a positive way. Such people do not have to turn to others for affirmation; they find affirmation within themselves. A positive self-concept results in a person with the self-confidence necessary to deal with others in a professional and productive manner. Customer service providers must work to develop a positive self-concept. Angry customers may take out their frustrations on the person who is trying to assist them in finding resolutions to their problems. When this happens, it would be easy for an individual with a poor self-concept to take the customers' words or actions personally. A positive self-concept creates the armor necessary to keep customers' actions in perspective.

◖ **self–concept** The way in which a person sees himself or herself and thinks that others see him or her.

Unfortunately, many people do not have a positive self-concept. Society places a number of unrealistic examples of perfection before us. The media continue to show us that in order to be truly happy we must be attractive, tall, thin, witty, affluent, and perfect in every way. This example sets many people up for disappointment. How can we interact with the world in a positive manner if we are less than what we see as ideal? This is a challenge that faces most Americans.

Others are not influenced by the example that the media have established but have been surrounded by negative people. Negative people can easily chip away at an individual's self-concept. If someone tells me that I am not good, why shouldn't I believe them? The most important thing that people with a less-than-positive self-concept can do is to realize that they alone have the power to change the way that they see themselves.

Methods of Improving Self-Concept

Every individual has the ability to improve his or her own self-concept. While others can affect how individuals see themselves, change must begin within the individual. The first step in improving oneself is to perform a self-assessment. A **self-assessment** is an individual evaluation in which individual strengths and weaknesses are identified. A self-assessment helps individuals to determine where they are headed if they make no changes in themselves or in their behavior. A self-assessment must be performed honestly and is meant to evaluate the individual. Instances in which individuals believe that they have been overlooked or have experienced "bad luck" are not relevant during a self-assessment. Excuses and blame do not contribute to the performance of an accurate self-assessment.

To begin performing a self-assessment, ask yourself the following questions and record your answers on a sheet of paper or on your computer.

1. **What are my strengths?** What do I receive compliments from others for having done well? What do I think that I am good at?
2. **What are my weaknesses?** What activities do I feel less confident in performing? Do I frequently make excuses or blame others for my failures? Do I finish what I start? Do I say yes too often? Do I pull my weight in a group activity?
3. **How do I see myself?** Am I dependable? Do I speak well in front of others? How is my sense of humor? What do I like most about myself? What do I like least? If I could change one thing about myself, what would it be?
4. **What are my likes and dislikes?** What kind of activities do I enjoy participating in? Do I like to sit in one place as I work, or do I like to move around? What subject did I enjoy the most while attending high school or college?
5. **Do I establish goals and work toward achieving them?** Do I take pride in successfully accomplishing a task?

It is not enough to perform a self-assessment. After assessment, the individual must evaluate the recorded information. When evaluating, it is helpful to draw conclusions and to develop a plan for the future. Review the responses that you recorded as you performed your own self-assessment. Are there specific areas in which you are pleased with your responses? As you draw conclusions about your strengths and weaknesses, recognize that the future will be much more productive if you consider your strengths and weaknesses in establishing goals.

Even if you were not entirely pleased with the outcome of your self-appraisal, you now have valuable new information about yourself. Most

◀ self-assessment
An individual evaluation in which individual strengths and weaknesses are identified.

people have very little self-awareness because it is sometimes difficult to recognize who we are and how others see us. It is much easier to make excuses for our failures and to blame our circumstances on someone else. Do not dwell on any negative information that your self-appraisal may have revealed. Go forward making goals to emphasize the positive aspects of yourself and exploring ways to improve those areas that need improvement. Above all, accept yourself as the unique person that you are.

"Success is achieving your personal best."
Elaine Harris

Ten Tips for Improving Self-Concept

When working on improving your self-concept, try the following 10 tips:

1. See yourself as a success: Every individual has a special contribution to make to society. Those individuals who see themselves as successful will as a result demonstrate more self-confidence as they interact with others. Seeing yourself as successful affects your actions. In most cases, you will behave as a successful person because in your mind you see yourself that way. By dressing the part of a successful person, you will also demonstrate to others that you pay attention to detail. A person who presents a sloppy or extreme outward appearance may send the message to others that he or she lacks credibility or is not able to fit in well with others.

2. Spend time with positive people: Positive people tend to share encouragement with those they spend time with. By surrounding yourself with positive people, you will be more likely to hear positive comments and to think in a more positive manner. Positive people see what *can* happen, not what cannot. An individual who looks at the bright side of life will remind us of our successes at times when we are having difficulty seeing them.

3. Eat right: One of the challenges of leading a busy life is the temptation not to eat the foods that will make us healthy. It is easy to become so involved in carrying out our responsibilities that we neglect our own health. If location or time restraints require that you frequently eat at fast-food restaurants, make the healthiest choices possible. Too much caffeine from coffee, soda, or candy bars can cause the body to experience high and low feelings. Try to drink six to eight glasses of water each day. Water will keep your body hydrated and help you to avoid the highs and lows that frequently result from too much caffeine. If the temptation to hit the snack machine at break time is too great, plan ahead by bringing nutritious snacks from home. Carrot and celery sticks, raisins, cheese, fruit, nuts, or low-fat crackers can help to keep you going until your next meal.

4. Break a task down into smaller steps: Sometimes it is difficult to dive into a project because it seems overwhelming. A good way to get started is to break the task down into several smaller tasks. If a quarterly report must be written, begin by creating the cover page. Then create the outline. Make the completion of the report a priority, but complete it a piece at a time. It also helps to become more organized. Make sure that your desktop, information system, paperwork, and message system are all organized so that you can operate at peak efficiency and follow through on the commitments that you make.

5. Get enough sleep: Most adults need an average of eight hours of sleep per night. Try to determine the appropriate amount of sleep for you. If you awake feeling tired, must always be awakened by an alarm clock, and tend to drag as the day goes on, you probably need more sleep. Try going to bed 30 minutes earlier each night for one week. If you are still tired, go to bed 45 minutes before your usual bedtime. By experimenting with different amounts of sleep, you should be able to recognize how much sleep your body really needs. Busy lifestyles may make it difficult to maintain a consistent sleeping schedule, but the benefits are worth it. A well-rested person usually has more patience, a greater attention span, and the ability to be more productive than someone who is tired. Feeling rested may help your self-concept to soar!

6. Reward successes: When you accomplish something that you are proud of, reward yourself! Most of us know when we have done a good job, but all too often we may forget to give ourselves a well-deserved pat on the back. Take yourself (and a friend) to lunch to celebrate, spend some time doing something that you enjoy, or smile with the satisfaction that you did something well. Some people find it helpful to keep a record of their accomplishments. This record can be a special file or list. Too many people focus on what they cannot do instead of what they can do. By acknowledging and rewarding our successes, we can recognize what we are good at and will have a sense of accomplishment.

7. Practice positive self-talk: Everyone talks to themselves occasionally. Unfortunately, what we say to ourselves is not always positive. By saying negative things to ourselves, whether out loud or silently, we reinforce negative thoughts and ideas. We may also begin to rehearse confrontations that we fear may occur. This may cause us to doubt our abilities and to focus too much attention on negative issues. Try talking positively to yourself. Talk out loud in your car or home and silently when around others. Tell yourself that you can handle the challenges that are placed before you. Be your own encourager! You can accomplish great things when you tell yourself, "You can do it!"

8. Do something for someone else: Doing something for someone else is often the best thing that we can do for ourselves. By helping someone else, we focus our attention on someone else's needs. Unselfishness has long been recognized as a boost to an individual's self-concept. Offer to help the new employee learn the ropes, hold the door open for someone, take a sick friend dinner, walk your vacationing neighbor's dog, or do that little something extra for a customer. Everything that you do for someone else gives you an internal reward. You feel good about having done something. Whether or not the act is ever repaid is unimportant. You did it; that is what counts!

9. Exercise!: More and more companies are recognizing the benefits of having fit employees. Even if your company does not have a wellness program in place, you can create your own individual fitness routine. When you exercise, the positive results include having more energy, fewer aches and pains, and valuable reflection time. Healthy employees tend to miss work less often and frequently approach challenges with a more positive attitude. Fitness counselors recommend that you always consult your doctor before embarking on a new fitness regimen. Finding the time to work exercise into your life may be challenging, but even a few minutes of stretching can be beneficial. A common time for exercise for professionals is in the morning. Fewer interruptions can take away the opportunity for exercise if the day has just begun. To begin incorporating exercise into your daily life, try walking instead of driving (if that is reasonable), take the stairs instead of the elevator, do stretching exercises at your desk, or take a nice walk with a friend or loved one after work. The exercise will help you to feel better both physically and emotionally.

10. Learn something new: It is never too late to learn something new. A new trend among adults is to embrace the idea of lifelong learning. Lifelong learning means that we never assume that we know all of the answers or that we are too old to appreciate new ideas. With the changes that are occurring in technology, we are seeing a need for additional training more than ever before. In addition to gaining new knowledge, learning something new allows us the opportunity to meet new people, explore new ideas, and add new skills to our resume. To begin to discover the learning opportunities around you, read professional publications, learn new software programs, enroll in classes at the local community college, pursue an advanced degree, listen to books on tape, or devote time to learning something that you have always wanted to know how to do. Even if your learning does not apply to your professional position, you are broadening your knowledge base, and that will translate into new confidence that you will take to work every day.

Power of Self-Motivation

Customer service is frequently a thankless job. Unfortunately, our customers usually come to us when they have problems or are upset. To achieve excellence in customer service, one must have the ability to review a situation and to motivate himself or herself. Behaviorists have studied motivation for many years, and some of their basic conclusions have a few key commonalties. The most obvious one is that we all have motivations that cause us to do what we do. It is commonly suggested that we individually have the ability to motivate ourselves. This is sometimes the only motivation that we are going to get.

So how do individuals begin to motivate themselves? The following seven steps may provide a good start:

1. Post quotations that you find motivating at your workstation so that you can see them throughout your day. If you surround yourself with positive messages, even the most challenging customer will have a hard time breaking your spirit.
2. Follow the tips for improving self-concept. By developing a strong self-concept, you will feel good about yourself, inside and out.
3. Set goals and strive to achieve them. By staying focused on your goals, you will be more likely to accomplish them and to have the satisfaction of achievement.
4. Read motivational books or listen to motivational books on tape. Look for opportunities to listen, whether while driving, taking a walk, or working out. The motivational message will stay with you after the tape is over.
5. If you are having a low-energy day, walk, talk, and act like you are full of energy. Before long you will forget that you were tired and will feel as good as you look!
6. Develop your sense of humor and let others see it. A good laugh can help both you and those around you to feel refreshed and motivated!
7. Have fun! Motivated people accomplish their goals, feel good about who they are, and enjoy life.

"Good friends are good for your health."
Irwin Sarason

By following these steps for self-motivation, you will embark on the positive journey to becoming and staying a motivated person. Serve as a motivator to others and they will in turn serve as motivators for you.

Teamwork

teamwork
Working together to improve the efficiency of the whole.

A recent *USA Today* article suggested that employees prefer working on teams to handling projects alone. **Teamwork** means working together to improve the efficiency of the whole. For many employees, the idea of teamwork is appealing because employees can experience a unified approach to projects or work that does not exist when all responsibility rests with one individual. Some of the reasons why employees prefer teamwork, according to a survey conducted for Dale Carnegie & Associates, are as follows:

- Indicated lower stress—72 percent
- Increased work quality—67 percent
- Improved attitude—67 percent
- Increased profitability—67 percent
- Increased productivity—66 percent

Teamwork does not work in every environment, but in those where it is appropriate, it can improve morale and result in a more positive and motivational work experience.

Methods of Saying Thank You and Motivating Others

Sometimes the most motivating action that we can share with others is to express our appreciation to them. Saying thank you does not have to be expensive, but it can have rewards that are beyond measure. While some companies do not recognize the benefits of expressing appreciation, many of the managers and companies that employees want to work for appreciate the tremendous power of recognition.

People need to see that their efforts are appreciated. Letting employees know that they have done a good job or that their extra attention in completing a project was noticed can be the motivating force that encourages them to keep up the good work. Many companies do not have the financial resources to allow or may have trouble justifying the expense of a monetary reward. Employees usually do not care how much a thank you costs, but they appreciate the recognition it implies.

Some inexpensive but meaningful ways to say thank you follow.

- Extend the lunch hour by 15 minutes.
- Bring donuts for the entire department to celebrate an individual's or group's special efforts.
- Send a personal note of thanks.
- Give the employee corporate tickets to a special event.
- Acknowledge employees' contributions in a department or company newsletter.
- Designate a casual day in the employee's honor.
- Allow the special employee to leave work early to beat rush hour traffic.

Most employees appreciate any gesture of appreciation, no matter what. The motivating force behind the thank you is that employees and departments know that their efforts are noticed. Employees feel more pride in their work and in their contribution to the overall efforts of a company that is glad to have them as a part of the team.

KEY TERMS

morale	self-assessment	teamwork
motivation	self-concept	wants
needs		

QUICK QUIZ

1. Most people are motivated by the exact same thing.   T or F
2. Humor is not a motivating force in today's workplace.   T or F
3. Our personal requirements are referred to as needs.   T or F
4. Wants have little relationship to needs.   T or F
5. High morale can result in absenteeism and high turnover.   T or F
6. People with a strong self-concept have to turn to others for affirmation.   T or F
7. "Bad luck" is a great excuse for a lack of achievement.   T or F
8. Individuals have the ability to improve their own self-concept.   T or F
9. Reading motivational books can help an individual increase his or her self-motivation.   T or F
10. Feeling appreciated does not significantly increase job satisfaction.   T or F

OPPORTUNITIES FOR CRITICAL THINKING

1. How can the use of humor aid in the motivation of employees?
2. What is the difference between needs and wants?
3. List some of your own needs and wants. Which needs and wants do you find the most motivating?
4. What are some of the motivating factors found to be common among adults?
5. Which motivating factors are the most important to you individually?
6. What factors can cause low morale?
7. Why do you think that so many people have a poor self-concept?
8. Perform your own self-assessment.
9. How can a healthy diet enhance an individual's self-concept?
10. What can be done to increase self-motivation?

SKILL BUILDING

Human Relations

The ability to interact effectively with and motivate others is an important skill to develop. By striving to improve human relations skills, customer service providers prepare themselves for positive internal and external customer experiences.

Discuss and determine an appropriate resolution to the following human relations scenarios:

- Your company prefers that all employees adhere to policies when responding to customer requests. A few months ago, you waived the policy and gave a customer an extension on her account.

Until today, you had forgotten about the incident. A different customer called to request an extension. When you denied the customer's request, citing the policy, the customer responded by saying that he knew you had waived the policy for the other customer. How can you respond to this situation and keep both the customer and your company happy?

- Recently you have noticed a morale problem in your own department. Employees are arriving late to work, are taking a lot of personal calls during work hours, and are complaining about things that previously were not problems. Since you have no real authority, how can you assist in improving morale and in making your department a nicer place to work?

- Last week you gave a customer the answer to a question. The customer was not pleased with the answer and left angry. Today, it came to your attention that the answer that you gave the customer was not correct. In fact, the correct answer is in his favor. How can you contact the customer and convey the correct answer while maintaining your own professionalism?

Ethics in Action

You have recently been hired to work in the Bursar's Office of the local community college. You believe that you were hired because you have the unique ability to convey empathy while also solving the problem at hand. Today you showed up for your first day at work. One of your new coworkers has just posted a sign that says, "Poor planning on your part does not constitute an emergency on my part." What should you do?

CHALLENGE # Prepare a Company Newsletter

Challenge Objectives

1. To personalize the student's understanding of customer service.
2. To provide an opportunity to actively illustrate an understanding of customer service.
3. To successfully present the completed newsletter to others.

Assignment

Prepare a company newsletter for the company of your choice. This newsletter should be creatively presented and should be filled with suggestions about how to improve the employees' customer service. Your newsletter should be a minimum of two pages and a maximum of four pages. Review the newsletters that you have received observing style, content, and layout techniques. Attempt to create a newsletter that you would be motivated to read.

Presentation

Present your company newsletter in letter quality form. Your newsletter should be typed (and illustrated if you choose). It should be creatively displayed to encourage reading. Your newsletter should include the following:

1. A recognizable logo (your own design or someone else's)
2. A newsletter name
3. At least one article related to customer service
4. Your name listed as the editor of the newsletter

Happy creating!

- **Helpful Hint:** Try using a desktop publishing or word processing program with a newsletter wizard to begin learning to create a newsletter. This is a good way to learn the program and to easily produce a professional document.

ANSWERS TO QUICK QUIZ

1. F
2. F
3. T
4. T

5. F
6. F
7. F
8. T

9. T
10. F

Leadership in Customer Service

From Chapter 9 of *Customer Service: A Practical Approach*. Sixth Edition. Elaine K. Harris. Copyright © 2013 by Pearson Education, Inc. All rights reserved.

Leadership in Customer Service

Remember This

The most valuable gift you can give another is a good example.

In this chapter, you will learn how to

- Define leadership.
- Perform a self-appraisal of your own leadership abilities.
- Differentiate between formal and informal leaders.
- List characteristics of excellent leaders.

- Demonstrate effective goal setting.
- Create your own job aids.
- Experiment with illustrating leadership without position in your own work setting.

Leadership Defined

The customer service industry is in great need of leadership. **Leadership** is the ability to influence others. The most recognizably outstanding companies are known for their excellent leadership. Excellent leadership is a requirement of any business providing products or services to customers. Leadership is not the automatic result of a title; it requires the development of effective leadership skills and practice implementing them. Leadership skills are developed through the dedicated effort of individuals to improve their own abilities and to blend their own philosophies with those of their organization.

No company can produce outstanding service unless the key managers are obviously committed to a positive customer service philosophy. Rules and policies are not the answer. Policies promote consistency, but they are not capable of influencing others in a positive way; and, when presented improperly, they may appear harsh and unfriendly. Leaders have a vision of what can be, and they share that vision with others around them. Excellent leaders serve as coaches, counselors, and positive examples. They have the skills to actually perform the work for which those they are leading are responsible.

Leaders must promote an interdependent environment. An interdependent environment is one that continually reminds employees that no one individual is responsible for an organization's success. Success comes as the result of the unified effort of all participants contributing to the whole. The idea of interdependency means that no one individual should have to carry all of the responsibility, with others reaping the benefits but not pulling their own weight. This philosophy is not instinctive. It must be created and perpetuated by the leaders of an organization. Anything less than an interdependent philosophy can breed a "that's not my job" mentality. When the leaders of an organization allow this mentality to set in, unity begins to fade away and disappears quickly.

Leaders demonstrate empowerment. They allow their employees to make a range of decisions to assist their customers. Excellent leaders train their employees to make decisions, which benefit both the customers and the company. Employees have confidence in their own abilities and are able to share enthusiasm and knowledge with customers without fear of making mistakes. By demonstrating interdependency, a vision for the future, and empowerment, excellent leaders create a culture in which excellence in customer service is the standard.

Customer service providers must serve as leaders for their customers. Through their interactions, they share information, character, values, and enthusiasm with customers. Customers need leadership just as much as employees do. Customers feel more comfortable with products and services, methods of billing, the sharing of special circumstances, and special needs if they are treated with respect by an individual who is

leadership The ability to influence others.

capable of leading them through the process to the next necessary step. Customer service providers have a tremendous amount of influence over their customers. All individuals in an organization must work to develop their own leadership skills so that they can be as effective as possible in their roles as leaders.

Know Thyself

Leadership begins in our own minds. We must first see ourselves as leaders, and then others will begin to see our leadership abilities. Leadership necessitates self-knowledge. Individuals must become aware of their own strengths and weaknesses. After identifying strengths and weaknesses, customer service providers can begin to overcome their weaknesses and to refine their strengths. A self-appraisal can be performed simply. By writing down strengths and weaknesses, customer service providers can determine a starting point.

To know yourself as a leader, ask yourself the following questions:

- How effectively do I relate to others?
- Do I practice excellent time management?
- What are my values?
- Is my knowledge level what it should be?
- Do I share my knowledge with others?
- Are my customers a priority to me?
- Am I willing to take risks?
- Do I establish measurable goals for myself?
- Do I willingly work toward department and company goals?
- Do I play mind games with my coworkers and superiors?
- Do I allow negative thoughts to cloud my attitude?
- Do I actively acknowledge accomplishments of others?
- Am I likable?
- Do I willingly go above and beyond the call of duty?

These are not the only questions that will help customer service providers to begin to develop a self-knowledge of their leadership skills, but they are a good place to start.

No one can change someone else. People may try, but, in reality, change must begin from within. A manager has the following motto hanging on the wall of his department: "I am responsible for my own success, no excuses!" This motto represents the manager's attitude toward the responsibility of each of his employees to change themselves.

The business world today is highly competitive. Fewer and fewer people are getting ahead because of whom they know. Advancement is more commonly based on an individual's proven abilities and desire to perform. Excuses do nothing but hold people back. Most of all, customers do not want to hear a customer service provider's excuses. Customers have enough of their own challenges. They want to interact with enthusiastic and well-trained customer service providers who can solve their problems.

Excellent leaders are self-confident. If others criticize them, they are willing to examine the area of criticism and determine whether the criticism is deserved. If it is, they make changes and grow stronger from the experience. People want to be around self-confident people. Those with self-confidence have found approval within themselves, so they are not seeking it from others.

Formal and Informal Leaders

Within any organization, several types of leaders exist. A common method of defining leaders is to categorize them as either formal leaders or informal leaders. **Formal leaders** have the authority and power of their official position. Formal leaders have been chosen by their organization to lead others. They may have been given special training to better prepare them for their roles as leaders. Formal leaders have a high level of accountability. Because the organization has selected formal leaders and has given them specific responsibilities, they are accountable to their superiors.

Informal leaders have no official authority but do have the ability to influence others. Informal leaders are not chosen by management to fulfill their roles as leaders. The people who interact with informal leaders have unofficially appointed them. Frequently, informal leadership is an assumed role. Either an individual has unofficially taken on the role of leader or others in a department, organization, or company have begun to think of and treat him or her as a leader. Informal leaders can either help or hurt the formal leadership of an organization. Informal leaders who do not support the goals of an organization or manager can undermine the efforts of the formal leadership. For example, they might use their influence to persuade other employees to be uncooperative or difficult. On the other hand, informal leaders who are supportive of the formal leadership and its goals can serve as motivating forces to encourage other employees to work together.

Both formal and informal leaders can contribute to the success of a customer service program. Formal leaders can create a culture that encourages excellent customer service. They can empower employees to make appropriate decisions and to serve as positive examples of what the company desires from employee performance. Informal leaders can also help to create a customer-friendly culture. In addition, they can motivate their coworkers to higher levels of professionalism, can improve morale, and can relate to coworkers in areas in which formal leaders may have difficulty.

The employees of a large utility company were experiencing a new philosophy in the way that management wanted them to approach their business. The leadership of the organization had always demonstrated the idea that their company was the only utility provider; therefore, the

formal leaders
Have the authority and power of their official position.

informal leaders
Have no official authority but do have the ability to influence others.

Job Link

Consider the formal leaders that you interact with in your daily life. *List five qualities* that describe the formal leader that you *most respect.* Think about how you could work to develop the qualities that you most admire in this person. Observing a positive leader can be a great way to develop your own leadership skills!

customers had to do business with them. This philosophy had resulted in a group of unmotivated employees who reluctantly came to work dressed sloppily, who complained about how unappreciated they were, and who basically thought of customers as a huge inconvenience. When technology allowed new competition to enter the marketplace, the management of the company had to change its philosophy on the level of customer service that it was willing to provide. Suddenly, the same managers who were casually approaching every aspect of their business were telling their employees about the importance of customer service. The employees were not interested in changing their behavior. They resisted change and envisioned retirement on the horizon. It seemed that no matter what the formal leadership of the company did or said, it fell on deaf ears.

Out of desperation, they turned to the informal leaders whom they recognized among their employees. They did have a few employees who had positive attitudes, who were excited about the new competitive approach to business, and who were highly influential with the other employees. These employees were invited to participate in updated customer service training and were encouraged to enroll in business courses at the local junior college. The employees were asked to help win over their coworkers—not in an obvious way but through their actions. While this approach did not have immediate results, over a period of time it did prove to be effective. It became accepted behavior to come to work professionally dressed and with a professional attitude. The company managers firmly believed that had it not been for the influence of the company's informal leaders, they would not have seen such a quick transition in attitudes and behavior of their employees.

Coach or Counselor

Leaders serve as both coaches and counselors as they lead their employees. They must be available to train, correct, and encourage their employees. In addition, they must help employees work through the challenges that may prevent them from doing their best work. We are exposed to leaders early in life. The earliest leaders in a child's life are his or her parents, teachers, and coaches. It is from that early exposure that many future leadership expectations develop.

Employees need excellent leaders. They need to have someone who will consistently show encouragement and who will help them to become successful. Good leaders have high expectations, and their employees want to do things well. Excellent leaders recognize that employees want to be noticed. They are observant of employees' efforts and notice when they are successful and when they are experiencing difficulty. Leaders know that sometimes employees gain more from experiencing failure than from always experiencing easy success.

As coaches, leaders recognize the value of delegation. Delegation involves assigning responsibility, granting authority, and creating accountability. To delegate a task to employees means that the employees know what they are supposed to do and are trained to do it. They are given the power to get it done. Finally, they are expected to do it. If they do not do it, they are confronted and required to give an explanation. Accountability is one of the hardest aspects of delegation and of leadership because many individuals find confrontation difficult. Confrontation does not have to be negative. It is simply an opportunity to obtain additional information and to remind an employee of what was expected.

Good leaders notice what is happening with their employees and in their business. They are aware when things are going well as often as they notice when things are not going well. They are quick to reward others with a compliment or another form of recognition. Leaders usually reap what they sow. If employees are treated well by their leaders, they will usually treat their leaders well in return.

As counselors, leaders are good listeners. They allow others to share situations and ideas. They do not interrupt. Openness to new ways of doing things is a welcome mat to new ideas and may cultivate creativity. When others share confidences, excellent leaders respect the privilege of the information and keep the knowledge to themselves. The unique combination of coaching and counseling allows a leader to assist others in achieving individual excellence.

Characteristics of Excellent Leaders

The characteristics that describe excellent leaders are varied. While everyone has his or her own definition of what it takes to be an outstanding leader, some characteristics are important to all definitions. Excellent leaders

1. Show care and respect.
2. Practice what they preach.
3. Have expertise in the area in which they are working.
4. Practice consistency.
5. Behave professionally.
6. Allow employees to do what they have been empowered to do.
7. Give support.
8. Demonstrate flexibility.
9. Make time for others.
10. Are personable.

Excellent leaders are not afraid to praise the work of others. Many salespeople and customer service providers will tell you that praise makes them feel confident and competent. Studies have shown that workers with only average ability had an increase in their quality of work after their manager began a concentrated program of praising their performance and of giving constructive feedback to them in an encouraging manner.

Author Joseph Klock of *Selling Power* magazine suggests the following guidelines for praising employees:

- Praise in public at every opportunity.
- Before you tell your people what you don't like about what they have been doing, tell them what you do like.
- Provide frequent feedback.

Not everyone who becomes a formal leader will demonstrate the characteristics that describe an excellent leader. These are the skills to be developed and refined to become an excellent leader. At different times, while interacting with different people, leaders discover that some characteristics may be easier to display than others. This is representative of the diversity of people and situations. An excellent leader always strives to be as effective as possible.

Leadership and Goals

goal An identified result to strive to accomplish.

goal setting The process of establishing goals and evaluating their importance.

Leadership requires finding the balance between what has to be done and who has to do it. This balance can be realized because of the establishment of well-defined goals. A **goal** is an identified result to strive to accomplish. Goals must be written down. Goals that are not recorded tend to become resolutions that are easily forgotten and are rarely accomplished. **Goal setting** is the process of establishing goals and evaluating their importance. To effectively determine goals, one must identify what needs to be accomplished. Goals can be established for small as well as large challenges. To record a goal effectively, follow these three steps:

1. **Write down the overall goal to be accomplished:** Goals should be as specific as possible.
2. **Identify how the goal may be accomplished:** What has to happen for the goal to be successfully completed?
3. **Include a date or time when the goal will be completed:** A deadline gives a timetable during which the goal is to be accomplished.

Just establishing goals is not sufficient. Goals must be constantly pursued so that they are accomplished. Some individuals find it helpful to record their goals on cards and to display them so that they are continually reminded of the goals that they are working to achieve.

The establishment of goals can serve as a motivator. The reminder that a goal is close to being accomplished can be the driving force that encourages a department or individuals to continue their efforts.

When establishing goals, it is helpful to begin with the end in mind. By recognizing the desired end result, individuals may be reminded of what is to come if the goal is achieved. In addition, their actions are more likely to stay on track, allowing them to be more productive. Goals are important in our professional and personal lives. Professionals should be familiar with the goals that their company has established for the organization. Professionals should also establish their own sets of personal goals. Personal goals should encourage personal growth, financial goals, and career advancement.

Sometimes one individual's goals can serve as an inspiration to others. A junior college student had a hard time making his college classes a priority; he enjoyed working and had a number of hobbies that distracted him from his studies. To help himself to stay on track and to accomplish the grades that he desired, he began establishing semester goals. His goals began small. The first semester, his goal was to stay enrolled in all of his classes for the entire semester. He successfully accomplished his goal, but his grades were not very good. The next semester, his goal was to stay enrolled in his classes all semester and to finish his classes with a grade of C or better. He again accomplished his goal. He began to see that he was succeeding in areas where he previously had not been successful. From this time forward, he established goals for each semester. Every time that this student accomplished a goal, he treated himself to an activity in which he had long desired to participate. He decided on the reward when he first established his goals. Because he had accomplished goals, he not only benefited from the original goal, but he had also gone hot air ballooning, become certified in scuba diving, and taken a hiking trip to the mountains; and the list went on! His reward system required that he also have a goal of having adequate finances available to pay for his reward, but that was a separate goal that he was motivated to accomplish. One semester during a class discussion on goal setting, he shared his method of setting semester goals with the members of his class. The other classmates were inspired by his accomplishments. They were also inspired by his reward system. By the end of the semester, he had several other students who joined him as he celebrated his post-semester reward of hang gliding. They had also accomplished their semester goals! Today, this student is a successful real estate agent and he is continuing to accomplish his goals.

◀ Creation of a Customer Service Culture

Leadership in customer service is illustrated through culture, which those in supervision create. **Culture** consists of the values, beliefs, and norms a group of people share. A customer service environment should have a customer service-oriented culture. If this culture does not encourage excellent

◀ **culture** Consists of the values, beliefs, and norms a group of people share.

143

customer service, then excellent customer service will not happen. A part of the culture that the leadership of an organization can inspire is the attitude of the employees. Leaders can inspire positive attitudes even when the chips are down and things are not going as well as desired. This is the time when employees are really watching their leaders. If the leaders demonstrate that they are fearful of what is happening and suggest that they think that things are out of control, others around them will begin to feel the same way. Customer service requires much more than a positive attitude, but attitude is an integral part of the process.

If the culture requires that customers be treated with respect, the result will be, in most cases, that the customers will be treated with respect. This also requires that those in leadership roles live according to the rules of the culture. Too often, the leaders of an organization act as though they are the only ones who deserve respect. When this attitude and behavior are an accepted part of an organization's culture, little respect will exist.

Additionally, if the leadership provides a safe environment for taking risks, efficiency and creativity will probably be improved. A positive customer service culture should show respect and concern for employees, be helpful in assisting in the problem-solving process, and provide positive recognition whenever possible.

Benefits of Job Aids

One of the common responsibilities of leaders is to provide training for their employees or coworkers. A well-trained workforce is one that is appropriately equipped to provide customers with excellent customer service. Unfortunately, one of the realities of training is that as time passes after the original training session, some of the knowledge may be forgotten. It is unreasonable to think that anyone could remember every detail of a training session, especially if he or she did not have the opportunity to use the knowledge frequently.

job aids
Leadership tools to reinforce training.

Job aids can assist in circumventing this problem. **Job aids** are leadership tools to reinforce training. Job aids can take a number of forms. They can be anything from a concise how-to-operate card posted on the fax machine to a list of "words to use" at every customer service provider's workstation. The important benefit of job aids is that they help people do things correctly the first time. Job aids are usually a combination of visual information and written information. They should always be concise and to the point. Unfortunately, Americans have a documented aversion to instruction manuals. This makes the value of job aids even more important. The user may never have been taught or never have read how to perform a procedure. A job aid can serve as a miniature training program.

Job aids are appropriate for both employees and for customers. Any situation in which a question may be asked concerning how to do something may indicate a need for a job aid. As technology continues to become a more important part of customers' lives, job aids will help them to actively take advantage of the technological opportunities. Job aids can remind users to use caution when operating dangerous equipment, and they can improve the safety of a work environment.

Many banks have added to their customer service offering by adding 24-hour automated account information lines. These telephone lines can provide customers with a considerable amount of information if the customers know how to operate them. If customers do not understand the operating procedure, they may get caught in a technological loop that will provide only frustration. To assist customers in using this technology, many banks send customers cards with the information line telephone number and with the specific numbers to press for the different types of account information. These cards can be posted near a telephone or can be carried in the customer's wallet for easy reference.

Job aids assist customers in being coproducers of their own customer service. Coproduction is when external or internal customers participate in providing at least a part of their own service. Job aids remind customers how easily they can do something. A large travel agency went to great expense to install a new telephone system. They invested additional money by providing extensive training for their employees so that they could use all of the features offered.

One month after the training was completed, a check was performed to determine which of the features was being used the most. Unfortunately, the results were discouraging. Almost none of the new features were being used. In fact, very few employees had even recorded their own voice mail messages. The managers were called in and told to go back to their employees and to find out why the system was not being used. After the employees were surveyed, it was discovered that although the employees were excited about all of the capabilities of the new telephone system, they could not remember how to perform all of the specific procedures. When the employees were working with customers all day, they did not have time to study the instruction manuals. After the management became aware of the problem, they created job aids to be placed on all of the telephones explaining the main functions and procedures. Usage went up almost 100 percent! When the employees could easily reference how to use the system, they began using it.

Job aids are helpful in aiding the recall of all of the following:

- Computer command and software usage
- Recommended telephone greetings
- How to operate copy machines, fax machines, modems, or specialized equipment
- Steps in a problem-solving process
- Telephone system usage
- Safety precautions
- How to file insurance claims
- Anything else that employees or customers have been trained or encouraged to do

The creation of job aids requires a degree of creativity. Leaders must look for opportunities in their own environments that could be enhanced by the addition of a supplementary leadership tool to reinforce training.

Leadership without Position

Unfortunately, in customer service, management and staff sometimes have an adversarial relationship. Those individuals who are supposed to act as leaders do not do so. In the area of customer service, all too often it is the managers who send their employees out to be trained in how to provide excellent customer service, while lacking the skills themselves. This can be discouraging for employees. In these instances, it is necessary for informal leaders to take a leadership role. This means that those employees who are respected by their peers and thought of as informal leaders can help to create an environment that encourages customer service, an environment that their managers may not be creating. This can be referred to as *leadership without position.*

Leadership without position may require a certain degree of assertiveness on the part of employees. Informal leaders or motivated employees can look for opportunities to share their leadership skills with others in an unofficial way. Any time that individuals interact in a positive manner, an environment begins to become more unified. If employees want to have a more positive influence in their workplaces, they can be the ones to get it started.

Some things that you can do to show your leadership are

1. Congratulate someone for handling a situation well.
2. Make suggestions to your supervisors of ways to help improve your efficiency.

TEAM TIME

Sit down with your team and discuss job aids. Remember, *job aids are leadership tools to reinforce training.* Think about ways that job aids could be used within your department or company. Job aids help people to do things correctly and serve as a *miniature training program.*

Create a creative job aid that will assist in the ongoing training of individuals within your organization. Think through all of the methods of explaining the information in your job aid. Try to make the job aid as simple and to the point as possible. This may require a few revisions. When you are satisfied that your job aid is creatively presented and accomplishes its goal, share it with your supervisors. You and your team may have designed an effective training tool that will benefit your entire company!

Happy creating!

3. Greet your coworkers with a smile.
4. Treat others as you would like to be treated.
5. Add your own positive method of showing leadership and encouragement.

Your Boss Is Your Customer Too!

One of the most challenging customers that you deal with each day may be your boss. Remember that your relationship with your internal customers is an important key to success in serving your external customers. Your relationship with your boss can make your professional life full of joy and reward or a daily-dreaded task. Successful customer service providers are already actively attempting to understand and to meet the needs of their other customers; why not include your boss in that group?

To begin to meet and exceed your boss's expectations, try the following:

- **Be a team player:** By allowing your boss to be the coach of his or her own team, you give him or her the opportunity to lead you to accomplish organization or department goals.
- **Find out what your boss considers to be important:** By identifying your boss's priorities, you develop an awareness of what he or she is striving to accomplish. You can then be of assistance in those specific areas.
- **Be a collaborator, not a complainer:** Nobody wants to be around someone who is always griping about something. If you disagree with how a project is being coordinated, share your ideas and take it in stride if your suggestions are not implemented. Never criticize, insult, or make fun of the boss to others. This is a reflection of your own bad attitude and others will recognize it. Being a part of the solution is much more positive than being a part of the problem.
- **Have reasonable expectations:** Your boss can only do what is within his or her power and ability to perform. In most work environments, several people report to their supervisor; therefore, you are not the only person your boss must consider when making changes or assignments.
- **Go to work each day with a great attitude and the willingness to be a professional:** Every individual must take responsibility for his or her own performance. Attitude plays an important role in how successful a person is in his or her professional life. In addition, the willingness to embrace new technologies and systems may be challenging at first, but it will usually ignite a new enthusiasm for the customer, the work, and hopefully even the boss.

Through excellent leadership, the management and employees of companies can more effectively serve both internal and external customers and can demonstrate that they are accomplishing the goal of providing excellent customer service.

KEY TERMS

culture   goal setting   job aids

formal leaders   informal leaders   leadership

goal

QUICK QUIZ

1. The most recognizably outstanding companies are known for their excellent leadership.   T or F
2. Leaders must promote an independent environment.   T or F
3. To be effective leaders, individuals must become aware of their own strengths and weaknesses.   T or F
4. Formal leaders have neither authority nor power.   T or F
5. Informal leaders have no real power, either official or unofficial.   T or F
6. Excellent leaders are not afraid to praise the work of others.   T or F
7. Goals that are not written down are usually achieved.   T or F
8. The values, beliefs, and norms a group of people share are their culture.   T or F
9. Job aids are mini training programs.   T or F
10. By congratulating someone for handling a situation well, an employee is showing leadership without position.   T or F

OPPORTUNITIES FOR CRITICAL THINKING

1. Identify five qualities of a good leader.
2. List and explain four things that can be done to show leadership without position.
3. Why are many of the companies that are recognized for providing outstanding customer service known for their outstanding leadership?
4. Explain an interdependent environment. How important is it?
5. How seriously should an organization regard its informal leaders?
6. List some characteristics of excellent leaders.
7. Why are so many individuals in leadership such poor leaders?
8. Have you seen individuals who establish goals accomplishing them? Do you set your own goals?
9. What is a job aid? Create a job aid that would assist your internal or external customers.
10. What does leadership without position mean?

SKILL BUILDING

Leadership

Most individuals need the positive influence that excellent leaders share with those around them. Excellent leaders become positive examples for others because they have recognized and have worked to refine their interaction skills. By observing individuals who demonstrate positive leadership, we can identify qualities to develop in ourselves.

Identify one individual who, in your opinion, is an excellent leader. List the qualities that this individual demonstrates as he or she interacts with others. Include such qualities as level of expertise, personality, and so on.

Now examine and list your own qualities as a leader. Even if you are not in a formal leadership role, you probably still possess leadership abilities. After listing your own leadership qualities, compare them with those of the excellent leader that you observed. Develop goals that can help you to enhance and improve your current abilities so that you can become a more skilled leader.

Ethics in Action

You are an assistant manager at a local bank branch in an outlying community. You walk into a "sister" branch of the bank to make a deposit. You don't know anyone there but as you are waiting in line you hear a torrid story, shared between tellers, of an affair that is supposedly taking place between the branch manager and another teller. Since you are fifth in line, you are not the only person that is hearing this story. What should you do?

CHALLENGE   Résumé

Every rising professional must at some point create a marketing piece that will help to sell him or her to prospective employers. That marketing piece is a résumé. A résumé is a powerful yet concise breakdown of your education, your job experience, and anything else that will illustrate for a prospective employer that you are the best candidate for a new job or opportunity. A résumé is not just about your past jobs; it is about *you*. An effective résumé is creatively written to emphasize your positive attributes and experience. Even a less-than-perfect past work history can be described in a positive way.

If you have never created your own résumé, the task may seem difficult and overwhelming. Numerous resources are available to assist you in the process. Your local bookstore or library will have books on résumé writing, and a search on the Internet can provide you with helpful information and examples. Services are available to create a résumé for you for a fee. While this may seem like an easy way to have a great résumé, it can be very costly and will not allow you to easily (and inexpensively) modify it for a specific position. You may also find out after you have paid for it that the résumé that you paid someone to prepare is not any more professional than one that you could have created yourself.

A few items to consider as you begin to create your own résumé are the following:

◖ Include your name. Avoid using nicknames. If your name may be considered unisex, include *Mr.* or *Ms.* to remove any question as to your sex.

◖ Include your address and phone number and use a number that would allow you privacy. (In other words, do not put your current work number if you are looking for a new job.) If you have a fax number, include it; and *definitely* include your e-mail address. Your e-mail address will show that you are using current technology and will give the prospective employer a quick way to contact you. If you include your e-mail address, make sure that you check your e-mail daily so that you do not miss out on an important message.

- Create and include a job objective that describes what type of job you are seeking. When you create your own résumé, you can easily change your objective as you apply for different types of work. Your job objective should be one or two sentences.

- Include your work experience in reverse chronological order. This means your most recent experience is listed first working back from there.

- As you list your work experience, include your title, place of employment, location of the company (town and state are detailed enough), and your dates of employment.

- Describe what your responsibilities were in each position. If you had several positions at one company, list them all as separate jobs.

- Wherever possible, list your successes in your position. If you helped to increase sales or saved the company money through a new method of doing business, include that in your description.

- If the title of your position does not describe what you really did, include the additional duties.

- If you have gaps in your paid employment history, include any positive details to cover the time span. If you were a student, a stay-at-home parent, a volunteer, or in another unpaid position, you can describe this in a way that shows you in a positive manner.

- If you are fluent in additional languages, have specialized computer skills, or have related activities or interests that help to qualify you for a position, that information should be included. Place this information in either the previous work experience section or in an additional information section.

- Include a listing of your educational background. This section should also be in reverse chronological order.

- Finally, on a separate page, list your references. You should always ask people if they are willing to serve as a reference for you before you list them. If they agree to serve as a reference for you, determine what address, phone number, and e-mail address they would like for you to use.

- Most reference pages include three or four references. Choose your references carefully; family members are not usually considered to be unbiased references.

- Always save your résumé on your computer or external drive so that you can use or modify it in the future.

Challenge Objectives

1. To collect the necessary information to create a professional résumé.
2. To organize and design your résumé.
3. To create a professional résumé that is appropriate for the area of employment in which you would like to work.

Assignment

Create a résumé for yourself. Consider all of the previously listed topics as you develop a résumé that is a marketing piece that will help to sell you to prospective employers.

Presentation

Submit to your instructor your completed résumé. Your résumé should be *perfect!* Proofread it several times and then have someone else review it. A professional résumé is always typed, is very readable, and does not have too many fonts or very large or very small print. You should have no misspelled words or grammatical errors. All sections should be parallel. This means that the same time arrangement (reverse chronological order) and the same style headings should be used throughout.

If this is the first résumé that you have created, congratulations! The first résumé is always the hardest one to write. Keep extra copies of your résumé and save it on your computer so that the next time you will just have to edit your work to update it.

◀ **Helpful Hint:** Microsoft® Word® has a great résumé wizard and several sample résumé styles that will allow you to fill in your own information for a professional résumé very quickly.

ANSWERS TO QUICK QUIZ

1. T	**5.** F	**9.** T
2. F	**6.** T	**10.** T
3. T	**7.** F	
4. F	**8.** T	

Customer Retention and Measurement of Satisfaction

From Chapter 10 of *Customer Service: A Practical Approach*. Sixth Edition. Elaine K. Harris. Copyright © 2013 by Pearson Education, Inc. All rights reserved.

Customer Retention and Measurement of Satisfaction

Remember This

A truly satisfied customer shall return!!

In this chapter, you will learn how to

- Define customer retention.
- Explain the value of existing customers.
- Define churn (or churn rate).
- Calculate churn rate, defection rate, and customer lifetime value.
- Identify how to tell if you need to improve your customer retention.

- List the steps for establishing a customer -retention program.
- Create your own list of ideas for evaluating your own performance.

What Is Customer Retention?

Customer retention is the continuous attempt to satisfy and keep current customers actively involved in conducting business. The importance of keeping current customers has been known for a long time. Interestingly, even though managers have recognized this fact, very few have created an active approach for keeping customers. Most businesses are focused on finding new customers, not on maintaining existing ones. Numerous businesses send salespeople out to make the initial sale and then leave customer maintenance to the customer service department. The trend today is to recognize the importance of those customers who have already made the commitment to do business with us and to create an environment that encourages those customers to continue to work with us.

Most individuals who work with customers know that it is much more costly to attract new customers than to keep the ones they already have. In spite of this knowledge, most companies do not have a plan specifically designed to maintain a relationship with existing customers. For many companies, the plan has been informal to the point of being nonexistent. Most customer service providers and salespeople know they need to be nice to their customers, but it takes a more deliberate approach to retain customers. Some companies follow up with their customers when business is poor and they are in need of additional income. This is a poor representation of a customer-retention program. A well-developed plan for customer retention creates an environment in which current customers' needs are met on an ongoing basis and new needs are explored. Customers are reminded by their experiences that they are valued customers of a company and, therefore, they have the desire to continue to do business with that company. Real customer retention consistently reminds customers that they are important. The result of customer retention is that customers will be so satisfied by a company that they are not motivated to seek other opportunities. They see that their dollars are well spent and that they are receiving a positive return on their investment. Customers also develop a stronger loyalty to those companies that show an interest in them.

Value of Existing Customers

Existing customers have a tremendous value! They know how our company approaches business. Existing customers know us and our policies. They are familiar with our products and services. They frequently buy without requiring a sales pitch. They will not tolerate a decline in our quality, but they will consider new product or service offerings more easily.

Our existing internal customers are especially important. We must work to maintain our internal customer relationships. Internal customers are frequently taken for granted. Because internal customers are the

◖ **customer retention** The continuous attempt to satisfy and keep current customers actively involved in conducting business.

"Become a partner with your customer, not just a vendor. The distinction is important. A vendor simply takes the customer's money and provides a product. A partner takes the customer's money and provides a "solution" that looks suspiciously like a "product" except it costs more."
Scott Adams

people we work with, it is difficult and sometimes impossible to find new internal customers. Internal customers may not be able to stop doing business with us, but they can become difficult to work with. Anything that unifies internal customers can have a positive effect on the success of a business.

Existing customers have the desire for our company and for us to expand our offerings. The more we can do for them, the easier it is for them to do business with us. All customers want to feel as though they are appreciated, even those cooperative customers who have never made a complaint. Unfortunately, it is easy to overlook those customers who are the most important to us. A customer who has done business with a department store for a number of years and who has a store credit card may resent the store's offering new credit customers a special discount on their first purchase if they open a new account. The long-term customers may or may not have received special incentives when they opened their accounts; but, if time has passed, the appeal of the initial offering has been forgotten. The long-term customers want an up-to-date display of the company's appreciation for their business. What can the department store do? Discount coupons, preferred customer mailings, deferred billings, and invitations to special events can be positive incentives. With the competition that exists in business today, there is always another company working to attract our customers' business.

Customer retention is not dependent on technology. Technology may assist in the process, but customer retention is really nothing more than common courtesy, showing customers that you care and appreciate them. Someone once said, "Don't date your customers; marry them." What were they talking about? If we "marry" our customers, we make a commitment. We let them know that we are in an ongoing relationship. We do not just show our positive qualities and hope that our weaknesses never show up. By "marrying" our customers, we show them that we are concerned with their success and happiness today and in the future.

As companies enter into financial commitments, which is what doing business is, they are weighing the reasons for committing their dollars. They want to know that they are getting a "bang for their buck." If they are not, they may choose to allocate their dollars elsewhere. One area in which the need for customer retention is especially important is in the area of nonprofit business. Businesses that seek donations or time from individuals must have a customer-retention program in place. Customers are becoming cautious about how and where they invest their money and time. If they do not see it going for a worthwhile cause or do not see that they are getting anything from the investment, they may redirect their spending. Few individuals would want to return to a social, civic, or religious organization that did not periodically say thank you or acknowledge their presence until they were gone.

"In a world where progress is measured in bits and bytes, advanced technology will never be able to replace the need for good minds, strong will, and unselfish hearts."

Clifton Taulbert

Understanding Churn

Marketing programs within established organizations, large and small, continue to focus on attracting new customers while the needs and desires of current customers are frequently neglected. What this approach fails to benefit from is the tremendous value of satisfying and retaining existing customers. A way to measure the significant value of retaining existing customers is to measure the churn rate, defection rate, and customer lifetime value for a given year. **Churn (or churn rate)** is the number of customers who leave a business in a year's time divided by the number of new customers in the same period.

$$\text{Churn} = \text{(number of defections)/(numer of new customers)}$$

This tells us that if 210 customers stop using a service and 350 customers purchase for the first time, there is a *60 percent* churn rate.

Defection rate is the percentage of customers who leave a business in one year.

$$\text{Defection rate} = \text{(customers who left)/(customers we had)}$$

If we began the year with 1,000 customers and ended the year with 350 fewer accounts, our defection rate is 35 percent.

Customer lifetime value is the net present value of the profits a customer generates over the average customer life.

$$\text{Customer life time value} = \text{(yearly profit)} \times \text{(customer life in years)}$$

If your average customer generates $3,000 in profit per year and your average customer life is 8.6 years, then your customer lifetime value before factoring in net present value is $25,800. Once you know how much it costs to lose a customer, you can make decisions regarding investments to retain customers. From this method of determining churn, defection rate, and customer lifetime value, it is easy to determine that even a small reduction in customer defections can result in positive profit results.

◀ churn (or churn rate) The number of customers who leave a business in a year's time divided by the number of new customers in the same period.

◀ defection rate The percentage of customers who leave a business in one year.

◀ customer lifetime value The net present value of the profits a customer generates over the average customer life.

How to Tell If You Need to Improve Your Customer-Retention Programs

If you do not have answers for all of the following questions, it is time to develop a customer-retention program within your company.

1. Are you measuring customer satisfaction?
2. What level of priority is being placed on customer satisfaction?

3. Do you measure quality standards and communicate results with management and staff?
4. Do you train and retrain customer service providers?
5. What is your level of employee turnover?
6. How much do you spend to keep current customers?
7. What is your cost for acquiring customers?
8. What is your customer-defection rate?
9. What do you do to get customers back?
10. Do you deliver on what you promised to your customers?

Development of a Customer-Retention Program

When developing a customer-retention program, it is important to create a program that is manageable and that supports the goals of the organization. Some of the most basic approaches to customer retention are follow-up phone calls, face-to-face visits, special events, name recognition, reminder faxes, coupons, newsletters, and the willingness to do a little something extra.

Customer retention requires initiative. It means that customer service providers must tune in to what the customer needs and be ready to suggest new opportunities. It also means that providers must cultivate relationships with customers and convey the message that the customer is more than just a business contact.

One company began its customer-retention program by implementing what was called "Fun Fridays." One Friday each month was designated as "Fun Friday." On "Fun Friday," every employee in the organization stopped what they were doing to call an assigned number of customers. The time allotted for calling was 10 minutes. The goal was to reach all customers by phone at least once in one year. The customer conversations were opportunities to ask the customers how they were doing, to ask if they had any special needs, and to let them know that their business was greatly appreciated. To add to the excitement of "Fun Fridays," employees were allowed to dress casually, were served donuts in the morning, and were qualified for prizes by participating. Everyone from the president to the mailroom clerks participated in calling customers on "Fun Fridays." An additional benefit of "Fun Fridays" was that those employees who previously had not had the opportunity to interact with customers began to feel as though they too had customer relationships. By allowing everyone to participate, no one individual or department had all of the responsibility for customer retention.

When establishing a customer-retention program, remember the following:

1. **Examine who your customers are and what specific needs they have:** If you understand who your customers are, a customer-retention program can be effectively created to cater to them and their business needs in an appealing manner.

2. **Identify specific objectives to be realized by the program:** Determine what is to be accomplished by the creation of a retention program. Objectives should be specific: to increase sales, to improve communication, or to enhance customer loyalty.

3. **Create a manageable program of customer retention:** Customer-retention programs should be manageable. They may need to start small and grow as they become successful and become a part of doing business.

4. **Create a culture that stimulates customer interest:** Management should provide an employee environment that makes it acceptable and appropriate to encourage customers to continue to do business with the company. Management should also provide active examples of management's philosophies in the managers' behaviors.

5. **Determine a timetable for evaluation:** When a customer-retention program is developed, it should designate a time at which an evaluation process will be implemented. At the time of evaluation, improvements can be made and successes can be recognized.

Measurement of Satisfaction

As we strive to provide customers with excellent customer service, we must periodically measure our customers' satisfaction. Customer satisfaction is the customer's overall feeling of contentment with a customer interaction. When attempting to measure our customer's satis-faction, expectations and perceptions must be considered. To measure satisfaction, frequent questions must be asked of many customers. The most common method of asking questions to determine satisfaction is through a survey. When preparing to create a customer measurement device, it is important to ask relevant questions that will provide an opportunity to generate helpful information.

When creating a format for measuring customer satisfaction, ask

- Who are the customers?
- How did they begin doing business with your company?
- Where are they located?
- Where did they conduct business with you (if there are multiple locations)?
- When did they conduct business?
- What did they like about the experience?
- How can we do a better job?

To effectively measure customer satisfaction, we must look at the customers' situations from their perspectives. A measurement format should be to the point and should not take more than a couple of minutes to complete. If it must be returned by mail, it should have a "postage paid"

Job Link

Share the concept of customer retention with a coworker (in case he or she is not familiar with it). Together, think of three things that you or your company could do to retain customers. Remember, customer-retention techniques do not have to be complicated. Now share your ideas with your supervisor and see what he or she thinks.

indication. Most customers will not seek out postage to mail a customer response unless they are very upset with our performance.

A discount store conducted a survey to determine what the customers liked or did not like about the store. The survey asked questions about the interior lighting, ease of finding merchandise, and prices and many other questions that would help provide better service to the customers. They did not ask anything about the parking lot or how safe the customer felt coming into the store. One customer responding to the survey had very positive responses to all of the questions about the interior of the store. When he or she was being thanked for participating in the survey, the customer asked if there were no questions to be asked about the parking lot. The survey administrator responded by saying that the parking lot was not important to the store at this time. This was not the right response for this customer! The customer shared that although there was satisfaction with everything inside the store, she was hesitant to come to the store after dark because of the inadequate lighting in the parking lot. There was also concern about the lack of identifiable handicapped parking spaces, the lack of lines dividing the parking spaces, and the number of stray shopping carts that could possibly damage surrounding cars. What this experience showed the company was that the original survey was not creating an accurate picture of how the customers felt about doing business with the company. Although things inside the store met the customers' expectations, the customers might not come inside because of the parking situation.

◖ Sources of Information

There are several sources for obtaining information about customers' satisfaction. The following list includes some possible sources:

1. **Informal surveys:** Informal surveys can provide insights about what customers like and dislike. Informal surveys may not be statistically measurable, but they can help businesses to know their customers better.
2. **Comment cards:** The use of comment cards is one of the most popular methods of determining a customer's satisfaction. They are easy to

create and are frequently available from company home offices. They do not provide detailed information, but they can provide immediate feedback. Customers may complete comment cards while they are involved in the customer experience.

3. **Verbal comments:** Verbal comments are easy to collect, but they are often ignored. By asking customers about their experiences, information can be obtained. To accurately collect information from verbal comments, employees must be encouraged to document comments on a customer log so that the comments are not lost.

4. **Historical data (point of sale):** With the use of computers in most workplaces, it is easy to collect historical data. To find out how much customers have purchased, how often they have purchased, and other related data, we can access the information at the touch of a button. Unless they are incorrectly entered, historical data can be very accurate resources for understanding customers. While historical data do not allow for emotion or opinions, they do give information concerning what is actually happening.

5. **Sales:** Like historical data, sales do not show emotion, but they do show what customers are currently doing. If they are increasing or decreasing orders, it will be reflected in sales. Sales are a good current indication of customer satisfaction, but they should be used in combination with other sources of information.

6. **Corporate-generated surveys:** Many corporations generate surveys that are sent to their customers. Corporate-generated surveys are usually more detailed than informal surveys, and the data that they reflect are usually statistically measurable. Corporate-generated surveys may ask questions about products as well as the service that was received. Corporate-generated surveys can collect a quantity of information, but they may have a lower response rate, depending on the customers surveyed.

7. **Discussions with internal customers:** Internal customers frequently have information about what customers like, do not like, and are interested in. If internal customers are never asked what their customers have told them, they may never have the opportunity to share their valuable information. Internal customers usually know what is not working well for customers and where snags in the system exist.

8. **Focus groups:** Focus groups are random groups of customers or prospective customers who are brought together to discuss current or future offerings of a business. Focus groups are sometimes challenging to coordinate, but they can cultivate a creative approach to understanding customers. Questions can be asked of the group and the responses can be recorded for future development.

9. **Toll-free phone numbers:** By providing customers with toll-free numbers to reach the company or department easily, we can encourage them to contact us when a question or problem arises. Toll-free numbers should be answered promptly by knowledgeable

employees who are well trained in answering customer questions and in responding to customer concerns. Some customers will call to share observations as they are occurring. These same customers may not take the time to convey their observations in writing. Customer comments should be documented so that they can be considered with other sources of customer information.

◀ **customer intelligence** The process of gathering information; building a historical database; and developing an understanding of current, potential, and lapsed customers.

10. **Customer intelligence information: Customer intelligence** is the process of gathering information; building a historical database; and developing an understanding of current, potential, and lapsed customers. The use of customer intelligence allows businesses to build on information already gathered and to add new information to get a total understanding of the unique customer relationship. When information already gathered does not have to be rediscovered, problem identification and solving can begin more quickly and affordably.

◀ Benefits of Measuring Your Effectiveness

Several benefits can be realized by measuring a company's or a department's effectiveness. By measuring effectiveness, weaknesses can be discovered so that corrections can be made. New customer needs can also be recognized so that new programs can be created and implemented to satisfy customers' current needs. Since customers may not share ideas and problems unless they are asked, the creativity of customers may go unnoticed. According to the *Harvard Business Review*, a 5 percent increase in customer retention yields about 25 percent to 125 percent increase in profits.

A wonderful benefit of measuring effectiveness is that we can discover what we are doing well. Customers are often quite satisfied by our offerings; but, unless they are allowed to share their satisfaction, the offering may be changed or updated to a degree that the customer may become dissatisfied.

◀ Tips for Realistically Determining Your Effectiveness

When attempting to realistically determine effectiveness, it is important to ask well-developed questions. Those questions should be asked of a variety of customers so that responses reflect a broad spectrum of customers. If a problem exists that is not going to be corrected no matter what customer responses are, it should not be presented to customers for consideration.

Explain why the questions are being asked. Express advance appreciation to the customer before he or she shares information. Thank the customer for having taken his or her valuable time to share responses. Explain that through the responses of many customers, the company can attempt to improve its services and continue with services that are currently meeting the needs of customers.

Why Surveys Do Not Always Reflect Reality

One of the most common methods of measuring customer satisfaction is through the use of surveys and comment cards. While these are the most common methods of measurement, they do not necessarily reflect a real picture of customer satisfaction. Frequently, the primary customers who take the initiative to respond to surveys and comment cards are those customers who are dissatisfied with their experiences or those customers who hope to gain from their comments. Satisfied customers may not take the time to express their satisfaction and therefore may not be included in the overall picture of satisfaction.

An additional problem with surveys and comment cards that may make them unreliable sources of information is the method of questioning that is used. This may be reflected in both the way that the questions are asked and the specific questions that are asked. Information may come back as being very positive, when in reality there are problems. Questions can be asked to avoid subjects that may receive negative responses. If a company has areas of customer interaction that are known by employees to be in need of improvements but upper management is not aware of them or upper management is being shielded from the information, these are areas that may never be addressed. Questions can be worded in such a manner that the information will not be revealed.

TEAM TIME

Sit down with your team and discuss *who* your customers are. Talk about what makes them unique. What do they have in common? What are their differences? Why do they continue to do business with your company? The different members of your team may have different ideas about who your customers are. These differences may be due to the different areas of the business that the members represent.

Now that you have identified who your customers are, create a short survey (10 questions or less) to share with them. Your survey should ask them questions about their level of satisfaction. Discuss the kind of questions that you want to ask so that you can clearly determine their satisfaction levels. You may want to focus on one specific area of your business. When you have your survey completed, share it with customers during a one- to-two-week period. At the end of that time, analyze the results.

While this will not be a scientific study, it can share some information with your company that it can benefit from. Any information that helps you to better serve and keep your customers is a good thing!

Surveys may not ask enough questions to establish valid information. A survey was circulated to establish customer interest in a new service that would be available for customer use after hours. The survey asked if the customers would like to see the new service offered. The survey results were overwhelmingly positive. The service was added. Unfortunately, very few customers ever took advantage of the service. The company was perplexed that the survey results could so overwhelmingly suggest that the service was desired and then have so few customers take advantage of its offering. A second survey was circulated to the same customers; the only addition to the original survey was the question "Would you actively participate in using this service?" The response was that almost none of the customers said yes. Upon further analysis, it was discovered that, although the customers thought that the service sounded like a wonderful idea, most did not believe that they would actually be able to use it. The omission of one question greatly affected the validity of the survey.

Ideas for Evaluating Your Own Performance

Sometimes the most effective method of evaluating customer satisfaction is to evaluate your own performance. If we examine the areas of our company and department that have the most questions asked, we may identify strengths and weaknesses without going to the customer. To evaluate your own performance, ask yourself these questions:

- Do my customers know that I am here to assist them with any questions that may arise?
- Am I well informed about the systems that my company offers to customers?
- Do I convey enthusiasm and interest to my customers?
- What skills could I develop that would enable me to better assist my customers?
- Do I practice name recognition and work at developing a relationship with my customers?
- What else could I do to assist my customers and department as we work to provide excellent customer service?

What Measurement of Satisfaction Means to Your Business

By measuring our customers' satisfaction, we deepen our relationship with our customers. We consider the customers' level of satisfaction, their expectations, and their perceptions. We ask questions and create an environment that encourages the sharing of ideas and concerns. The message that is conveyed to customers is that our company is interested in knowing what they think and is willing to actively strive to satisfy them. The seeking of feedback from customers can in itself result in positive customer retention.

KEY TERMS

churn (or churn rate)   customer lifetime value   defection rate
customer intelligence   customer retention

QUICK QUIZ

1. Customer retention is not as important as attracting new customers.   T or F
2. Customers develop a stronger loyalty to those companies that show an interest in them.   T or F
3. Existing customers will accept a decline in service without question.   T or F
4. Customer lifetime value is the percentage of customers who leave in one year.   T or F
5. Customer retention involves conveying to the customer that they are more than just a business contact.   T or F
6. When establishing a customer-retention program, it is important to examine who your customers are and what specific needs they have.   T or F
7. When measuring current customer satisfaction, the upcoming advertising campaign is an important consideration.   T or F
8. Informal surveys are statistically measurable and are therefore an extremely reliable source of information.   T or F
9. Focus groups are random groups of customers or prospective customers who are brought together to discuss current or future offerings of a business.   T or F
10. Seeking feedback from customers will never result in positive customer retention.   T or F

OPPORTUNITIES FOR CRITICAL THINKING

1. List five sources of information that would give insights as to the quality of a business's customer service.
2. Define customer retention.
3. What is the one thing that you and your company could do to retain your current customers?
4. Why is maintaining existing customers so important?
5. How do you measure churn or churn rate and why is it an important number to know?
6. What are some guidelines to consider when creating a customer-retention program?
7. Create your own device for measuring customer satisfaction. Try to limit it to 10 questions or fewer.
8. Verbal comments from customers are sometimes the easiest to get. Why are they not always the most accurate measure of customer satisfaction?
9. What are some questions that can assist an organization in evaluating its own performance?
10. Why should all customer service providers develop their own philosophy of customer service?

SKILL BUILDING

Customer Retention

The value of existing customers is greater than what many organizations realize. Unfortunately, most organizations direct the majority of their customer efforts toward new customers and therefore do not effectively meet the needs of the customers they already have.

Customer retention is the continuous attempt to satisfy and keep current customers actively involved in conducting business. Customer-retention efforts do not have to be expensive and are frequently not dependent on technology. The best customer-retention programs start small and encourage communication while reminding the customer that the organization is still out there ready to serve them.

Either individually or in a small group, list 10 creative elements that would seek to keep current customers involved in your business. Your ideas should reflect the specific customers that you interact with and their own unique set of needs and circumstances.

1.
2.
3.
4.
5.
6.
7.
8.
9.
10.

After recording the creative elements that would seek to keep current customers involved, rank them according to how easy they would be to implement.

By exploring the customer-retention ideas that you have recorded, you have established the basis for a customer-retention program. Share your ideas with others in your organization and begin the process of retaining customers!

Ethics in Action

Your coworker, Vicki, is having a bad day. She is being short with customers to the point of rudeness. Should you bring it to her attention, share the observation with your supervisor, or do nothing?

CHALLENGE Write Your Own Philosophy of Customer Service

There are as many different interpretations of customer service as there are individuals. Although businesspeople and customers are talking about the importance of customer service, many have never defined for themselves or for someone else what they believe customer service to be. Customer service providers must combine the knowledge that they have acquired about customer service with the realities of their professional environment. This definition of customer service becomes your individual philosophy. A philosophy is the combination of the ideas and convictions of an individual. In customer service, a well-developed and realistic philosophy can be the key not only to success in the industry but also to differentiating between individuals when they are applying for employment or are candidates for advancement.

Challenge Objectives

1. To allow students the opportunity to develop their own philosophies of customer service.
2. To integrate the students' up-to-date knowledge of customer service with their own experiences and day-to-day realities in the industry.
3. To convert ideas to words successfully and concisely.

Assignment

Consider the knowledge that you have acquired about customer service. Combine this knowledge with the practical experiences that you have had in customer service situations (both as a customer and as a provider). Compose in written form, as concisely as possible, your philosophy of customer service. Your philosophy should include (1) how you define customer service and (2) what you believe about customer service. Include any pertinent examples and any other information that supports your position.

Presentation

Prepare your philosophy of customer service in written form. Remember, your philosophy of customer service is completely your own. You may include specific definitions and ideas that were discussed, but it should also include other specifics as to why you believe what you do. Be concise.

ANSWERS TO QUICK QUIZ

1. F	5. T	9. T
2. T	6. T	10. F
3. F	7. F	
4. F	8. F	

Technology and Customer Service

Technology and Customer Service

CHAPTER OBJECTIVES

In this chapter, you will learn how to

- Identify some of the ways that customers of the twenty-first century search for and make purchases.
- Recognize customers' expectations of service providers.
- Explain some of the most rapidly advancing technologies that customers are seeking out.

- Express an understanding of what a call center is and some of the new trends in call center management.
- Explain teleselling.
- List the new ways that customers are doing business over the Internet.
- Understand the balance of serving customers using traditional and technological methods.

Today's Changing Marketplace

Today's marketplace is full of changes. Opportunities that seemed possible only in the distant future are now upon us. Suddenly emerging are Facebook, Twitter, YouTube, communication by texting, blogs, membership/reward programs, e-mail, and the list goes on! Customers are embracing these new opportunities with an enthusiasm that sometimes exceeds business's ability to deliver. In addition, customers may expect businesses to offer services that they are not quite ready to offer. This results in either offering services ahead of schedule or not offering them and being perceived as behind the competition. Increasingly a customer's first attempt to gain information about a product or how to use it is by way of Google or other search engine.

Social media is electronic communication used by consumers to share ideas, information, opinions, and personal messages. Customer service offerings are now being offered by way of social media. Social media is pushing companies to reevaluate and redefine how they serve customers. Some companies are using social media as a less expensive replacement for traditional advertising. There is virtually no cost associated with having a Facebook or Twitter account. No cost *initially* but as usage increases and the expectation of a more professional appearance, quicker response time, and increased functionality goes up so will the expense of the offering. The increase in the use of these methods of communication with customers may be a reflection of the economic downturn or a fundamental shift in technology. Regardless of why a company has chosen to communicate with the customer in this way, the reality is that social media has become a part of the ever-changing opportunity to serve customers.

Social media, on one hand, provides the chance for companies to have increased collaboration for problem solving. On the other hand, customers no longer complain in private. This reality gives customers increased power when seeking resolution to a problem. An offering that is neglected may bring negative attention to a business. For example, a Facebook page that a customer is encouraged to "Like" and then never has any new postings or status updates may do more damage than not having the page at all. Customers may start to wonder what else in the business has been forgotten. When using social media to interact with customers it is helpful to remember the following:

- Express appreciation to customers for referrals. Congratulate them on successes or new opportunities and affiliations.
- Share information, not a heavy sales pitch.
- Use status updates to remind customers of upcoming deadlines, events, and opportunities.
- Link to other resources whether offered by you or not. Especially, YouTube videos, articles that mention your business or product, important links, etc.
- Share what is trending in your market, such as, books, products, topics, new information, and interesting tie-ins to your business.

◀ social media
Electronic communication used by consumers to share ideas, information, opinions, and personal messages.

A chain of pizza restaurants with an enormously successful delivery system introduced its own website to handle orders, customers' comments, and complaints. This step was as a result of repeated customer requests although the company management was doubtful as to whether the website was needed, would prove profitable, and would enhance the already-successful delivery business. Customers liked the novelty of logging on to complete one more transaction in their busy lives. Customer usage increases daily, and as time has passed the efficiency of the website has increased. More and more businesses are being faced with this kind of decision—to introduce a service that optimizes current technology or to refrain from introducing it and seem behind the times. As time has gone by, since this initial introduction, the company has added menus online, couponing programs with coupons delivered via e-mail, and even a blog which encourages customers to share their favorite memories of eating this unique pizza.

Today's customers are intrigued by using new technologies to enhance their lives. Businesses have the challenge of identifying which technological opportunities their specific customers desire and how to deliver them in an easily usable fashion. Businesses must determine which technologies will bring about the desired customer result. Additionally, they need to analyze how much human power is needed to keep the technology current and up to date.

"As we go forward, I hope we're going to continue to use technology to make really big differences in how people live and work."

Sergey Brin

Understanding the Customer of the Twenty-First Century

Customers in the twenty-first century are sophisticated in the ways that they search for and make purchases. They expect the following from service providers:

1. **Availability:** Services are designed to meet the customer's schedule.
2. **Accessibility:** When the customer needs to talk, the provider can be reached.
3. **Accountability:** Customers prefer quick and accurate answers to service questions.

Source: Charlene Taylor, *Rural Telecommunications* magazine (November–December 1996).

Customers want hassle-free customer experiences that are user friendly and that validate customers' choices. Customers want to feel as though they are highly valued and that service responses are available when they *really* need them. Customers have busy lives today and will continue to have them. It is unlikely that customers are installing software for home use or will need to ask lawn mower repair questions during the hours of nine to five Monday through Friday. Finally, customers want to have service experiences that provide accurate answers in a timely manner. They expect increasing levels of accountability from the organizations they enter into business with. Surveying customers is not enough to discover their preferences. Customers expect the opportunity to offer their suggestions.

A new marketing strategy is being offered in several metropolitan areas that promises "Hassle-Free" automobile purchases and accessible service, and is described as "Car buying for the new millennium." When a customer recently called to make an appointment for an oil change, he was told that noon was not a good time to bring his car in, because the oil change technician would be at lunch. When the customer expressed that he needed to take care of this errand during his lunch hour, he was told that perhaps *the customer* could take a late lunch! The customer then stated that he *could* take his car to the oil change specialist down the street and that the specialist was *never at lunch*, the price was *cheaper*, and the car would be returned with the *windows washed* and the *interior vacuumed*. The customer did make an appointment and hung up. After thinking about his choice for a while, he decided that he would take his car to the other company for the oil change. When he called the dealer back, out of courtesy, to cancel his appointment, the on-hold message spoke of how the company was created to serve the customer. After several times of hearing the message and still being on hold, the customer hung up, frustrated and angry about how out of touch the company was with real customers. This is a perfect example of a company that is talking about service but obviously does not have a clue as to the real needs of its customer. Customers no longer stand for this kind of treatment. They take their business elsewhere; then, when companies feel the loss of customers, they all too often blame the economy or state that there is too much competition for the limited customer base. Customers expect enhanced service opportunities and do not settle for less than what meets their ever-changing needs.

"Technology shapes society and society shapes technology."
Robert W. White

Embracing New Technologies

Technology is progressing at a rate that is staggering. Customers are anxious to experiment with new technological options with the hope that they will be of benefit to them in some way. One possible reason that customers are more responsive to new technologies is that they have become, in many cases, very user friendly. As it becomes easier to understand and work with a system, people are drawn into using it. The positive benefit of this trend is that the standard of excellence is raised and, in most cases, the speed at which business is conducted increases. Some of the most rapidly advancing technologies that customers are seeking out and using are customer service call centers and customer service over the Internet, including online bill paying, buying and selling of goods and services, online tutorials, webinars (online collaboration or training), technical assistance, and e-mail. Smart phones are helping customer service to be "on the go," and the ability to acquire knowledge is highly portable.

When new technologies are introduced in the workplace, they are often greeted with a mixture of emotions—everything from enthusiasm to terror! New technologies mean new things to learn and old habits to break. To prepare others to greet the opportunities of new technologies with an open mind, take the following steps:

- **Prepare your staff:** Get the call center staff involved from the start.
- **Train supervisors and team leaders first and get them to buy in.**
- **Develop a group of "change champions" who will act as advocates for the new technology.**
- **Sell your vision:** Convey your enthusiasm and share how much easier work will be.
- **Praise successful use of the new technology.**
- **Resist the temptation to complain.**
- **Celebrate small successes:** Celebrate small milestones along the way to keep all involved excited.
- **Avoid the "shelfware syndrome":** The temptation to give up and put the new technology on the shelf, never to be used.

Source: Dr. Jon Anton, Customer Service Manager's Letter (May 10, 1998).

◖ Call Centers

> *"Any sufficiently advanced technology is indistinguishable from magic."*
>
> Arthur C. Clarke

One of the most dramatic growths that has been seen in customer service is the service offered via the customer service call center. Call centers have a unique advantage when delivering customer service. They can be located just about anywhere that has a sufficient worker base, and one call center site may handle a number of different companies' calls. Customers are accepting a little less one-on-one service for the increased convenience of being able to talk to a call center. Call centers allow service costs to be reduced from the costs resulting from face-to-face encounters.

A current trend in call centers is to locate them in foreign countries with eager workforces that are accustomed to a much lower rate of pay than the average American worker. Companies are still weighing the benefits of this business practice. From a cost basis, it can appear to be very beneficial to the bottom line; but customer satisfaction has in many cases suffered. Companies currently have to weigh the cost benefits against potential customer losses. Internationally located call centers incorporate extensive training programs to prepare their employees to professionally interact with American customers. These employees may even be given American-sounding names and biographies so that they can more easily interact with their American customers. When this approach to a call center is successful, the customer has no idea that they are not interacting with a customer service provider "just around the corner."

◖ **teleselling** Selling products, services, or information via the telephone.

Call centers include the category of teleselling. Previously referred to as telemarketing, **teleselling** is selling products, services, or information via the telephone. Two types of calls fall within the area of teleselling. **Inbound calls** are calls that originate with the customer and may include catalog ordering, billing questions, technical support, product use, or other information. In many cases, inbound calls are being replaced by online ordering, which may decrease the number of customer service providers needed to answer the phones. **Outbound calls** are calls that originate from the call center to the customer and are usually intended to sell products or services, conduct market research, or respond to customer inquiries. Many call centers handle both inbound and outbound calls.

Most customer service call centers have sophisticated telephone systems that include special call routing or **automatic call distribution**, which allows calls to be routed to the next available service provider. They may be linked to a **"call me" Web browser** feature that allows customers linked with a company's Internet site to be referred to a call center representative. The call center representative then calls the customer to respond to the customer request.

Automatic number identification allows the call recipient to identify the incoming number and caller. Additional background or historical information may be displayed on the recipient's computer screen to enable him or her to better serve the customer.

The call center workplace is a fast-paced environment focused on serving the customer as quickly and professionally as possible. The call center is not for everyone; however, those individuals with excellent telephone skills, ability to handle stress, good computer skills or the aptitude to learn new computer systems, ability to stay at their workstation in front of a computer, enthusiasm, positive attitude, motivation, good problem-solving skills, professionalism, and the ability to see a call through to the end would be excellent candidates for call center positions. Because of the importance of telephone skills, many candidates are interviewed by telephone to identify their telephone techniques.

◖ Customer Service Over the Internet

The growth of the Internet has exceeded most of the experts' predictions. The importance of the Internet in the area of customer service is dramatic. So many customer services can be offered via the Internet that companies must attempt to identify whether or not a website would enhance their service offering. A website could offer product and company information, new products, ordering options, answers to commonly asked questions, owners' manuals, part reorders, and technical updates—and the list goes on and on. Since so many customers have grown to expect company websites, many companies have been forced to create them. In some cases, their introduction is expensive and premature. A poorly designed website is frequently a bigger mistake than not having a website at all.

◖ **inbound calls** Calls that originate with the customer and may include catalog ordering, billing questions, technical support, product use, or other information.

◖ **outbound calls** Calls that originate from the call center to the customer and are usually intended to sell products or services, conduct market research, or respond to customer inquiries.

◖ **automatic call distribution** Allows calls to be routed to the next available service provider.

◖ **"call me" Web browser** Allows customers linked with a company's Internet site to be referred to a call center representative who then calls the customer to respond to the customer request.

◖ **automatic number identification** Allows the call recipient to identify the incoming number and caller. Additional background or historical information may be displayed on the recipient's computer screen to enable him or her to better serve the customer.

Some additional Web-based services that customers are engaging in are as follows:

◀ **online bill paying**
Offers customers the opportunity to receive and pay bills online.

◀ **Online bill paying.**   Numerous companies and banks are offering customers the opportunity to receive and pay bills online. This involves some initial setup, but it can greatly expedite the tedious process of bill paying for customers. For vendors, it can cut out paper, printing, and postage expense. For customers, it decreases the time that the bill-paying process may take and saves on check writing and postage expense. It also may mean a greater likelihood that bills will be paid on time. Increased customer satisfaction is a very positive benefit of the online bill-paying opportunity. Companies that do not offer this customer option may be perceived as behind the times and not as technologically advanced.

◀ **Buying and selling of goods and services.**   Online shopping is at an all-time high. In the early years of Internet shopping, customers told horror stories of how high postage expenses were and how products that were thought to have been ordered were really out of stock or on back order; and customers were fearful of giving out credit card information over the Internet. Most of these issues have been rectified. Customers today happily search out the best price and style options, thereby saving them time in not having to shop the local shopping mall. Most major retailers depend on the volume of sales that their online divisions create. Companies like eBay have enabled customers to buy and sell on their own without using the normal online retail approach. Setting up special payment accounts or using virtual credit cards has gone a long way in easing customers' fears of having the wrong person obtain their credit card information. Fraud is still a great concern for anyone using the Internet. Customers should always show caution when they are using the Internet and should not give personal information out without ensuring that they are working with a secure site.

◀ **Online tutorials.**   Companies can offer expanded training programs, operating instructions, and any other needed instruction through the use of online tutorials. Customers can access these tutorials at all hours and can in many cases repeat them until they are comfortable

---

Job Link

Explore what bills you may be able to pay via the Internet. Go to both the company that you do business with and your bank. Find out which method of bill paying has the least additional charge or, hopefully, no extra charge and is the easiest to coordinate. Create your own pro/con sheet to determine whether or not this method of bill paying is appropriate for you. If you already participate in an online bill-paying program, way to go! You are already using technology to enhance your life!

with the information. Answers to frequently asked questions (FAQs) may also be addressed in an online tutorial format.

- **Webinars** (online collaboration or training). Companies are using this new approach to training and information sharing. By using the Internet, specialized training can be delivered to a select group of customers. Training programs can be delivered without requiring the participants to travel, therefore saving money for the organization while improving skills.

- **Technical assistance.** A harsh reality of a technically advancing marketplace is the need for technical assistance. Sometimes technical assistance is delivered using a combination of the preceding approaches. Companies of all types can offer customers the opportunity to learn more about how to use a product or have questions answered via the Internet.

- **E-mail.**

webinars Online collaboration or training.

Call centers can provide considerable information and assistance to customers. A website can supplement what the call center is doing. Because so many consumers now have Internet access and actively use it, it makes sense that they would try a Web search to gain information or assistance from a company before they would track down a 1-800 number. By offering information via the Internet, companies may cut down on-hold times for customers with inquiries that could be answered via the website. In this respect, the telephone call center and the Internet can complement each other.

Most Internet sites have e-mail links that provide one more customer service. While this does give customers the opportunity to ask individualized questions, it can provide the opportunity for service failures. Customers that communicate via e-mail are actively seeking responses to their specific questions. While the website is largely impersonal and somewhat generic, e-mail questions are not. Some studies suggest that customers expect an e-mail response faster than a voice mail message. Some companies have found themselves faced with needing to respond to many more e-mail inquiries than their staffing will allow. Additionally, if a customer has conducted a search and has found your company as a possible provider of a product or service he or she is seeking, it is almost certain that he or she is looking at other similar companies offering similar products or services.

A customer seeking a provider of online stock trading services conducted a search to identify the companies that were offering this service. This search located several such providers. Two appeared to have the variety of services the customer was seeking. He then e-mailed the same set of additional questions to both companies. One company responded within three hours, apologizing for taking so long to respond. The other company took approximately four days to reply, included no explanation of why it took so long, and then provided vague answers to the questions. With whom do you think that the budding investor ends up doing business?

TEAM TIME

Sit down with your team and discuss *how* your company uses technology to serve your customers. Make a list of the different techniques that are in use. Then answer these questions:

1. Are all coworkers well trained in all technologies?

2. Do our customers understand how to participate in the use of these technologies from their side?

3. What additional technologies could we incorporate to better serve our customers?

Compile your findings and share them with your supervisor. You may share something with your supervisor that he or she had not thought of or that is in the works for your company.

Enhancing Service Experiences and Building Customer Loyalty

With all of the new opportunities that await companies offering customer service, it would seem that all a company would have to do is to offer the emerging services. As we go forward into the twenty-first century, customers are looking for more. Customer loyalty will be one of the defining areas of success or failure for service providers. This is one area that has been facilitated by communication methods like Facebook or frequent e-mail updates. Getting a business name in front of the customer as often as possible may increase loyalty. Due to the large number of service providers and the diversity of services offered, customers will be exposed to different ways of serving the customer. Every service interaction is an opportunity to better understand customers and to build a relationship with them. If handled properly, that relationship becomes a loyal one in which customers come to think of the company as the only one for them and then continue to vote with their business.

KEY TERMS

social media

automatic call distribution

automatic number
   identification

"call me" Web browser

inbound calls

online bill paying

outbound calls

social media

teleselling

webinars

QUICK QUIZ

1. Customers are not really interested in using new technologies in their customer interactions.   T or F
2. Customers are happy to take time away from their jobs during the week to have a lawn mower question answered.   T or F
3. Praising employees' use of new technology will help them to gain confidence. T or F
4. The location of call centers in foreign countries has always worked well in providing customers the best possible service.   T or F
5. Inbound calls originate with the customer service provider.   T or F

6. Automatic call distribution allows calls to be automatically routed to voice mail. T or F
7. Online bill paying is a big hassle that customers do not really want anyway. T or F
8. Customers trust the companies they do business with over the Internet and are therefore not concerned about fraud. T or F
9. Internet telephony is the same as wireless Internet.   T or F
10. Customer loyalty will be one of the defining areas of success or failure for service providers.   T or F

OPPORTUNITIES FOR CRITICAL THINKING

1. Describe some of the ways that customer service offerings are changing.
2. What are the three things that customers will expect from customer service providers as we move further into the twenty-first century?
3. Review the steps to prepare others to greet new technologies with an open mind and discuss your own reaction to the introduction of new technologies.
4. Explain the difference between inbound calls and outbound calls.
5. Discuss how many times you have called a 1-800 number in the last year and your expectations of the experience.
6. Conduct and tape-record a mock telephone interview. Listen to the tape and complete a self-assessment as to whether you would be a good candidate for a call center position.
7. Conduct an Internet search and, if possible, e-mail a question to two companies offering a similar product or service.
8. Compare the results and share your observations with others.
9. Give examples of businesses that could benefit from a website to supplement their customer service offerings.
10. What elements do you consider to be the most important in building customer loyalty?

SKILL BUILDING

Technology Training

Technology is an important part of our lives today. Unfortunately, most Americans do not take advantage of the opportunity to maximize the technologies they already possess. Consider how many times you have purchased a new television, DVD player, computer, printer, software package, camera, or other new technology and just started using it without reading the owner's manual. All too often, the only time that we consult the owner's manual is when something will not work or breaks.

Identify a product or service that you already own or have available to you. Read the owner's manual (or specific parts) and learn how to use some feature of it that you have not previously known how to use.

Now share the information with someone else who can benefit from the information. You may be surprised at how easy it is to learn a new technology when you read the instructions!

Ethics in Action

You have recently joined Facebook and are having fun connecting with old friends and new. Your company has a strict "no Facebook" policy at work but no filters are in place to block your access and to your knowledge no one really checks up on it. The two coworkers next to you have numerous personal calls everyday. You never have personal phone calls. Is there any real harm in logging in to Facebook at your desk and just minimizing it most of the time? After all, you aren't wasting time on the phone!

CHALLENGE   Current Events

Reading professional publications is an outstanding way to increase your understanding of new trends in business. This is also true in the area of customer service. Numerous articles are written on the subject. These articles may be found in newspapers, business periodicals, customer-service-specific publications, and at various locations on the Internet. Reading these articles is a good start to increasing your knowledge. Learning how to interpret the information included in articles is an additional skill. The completion of current event forms can begin the process of teaching individuals how to consider the facts in the article and then reminds them to consider their own thoughts and opinions on the topics covered.

Challenge Objectives

1. To locate sources for current articles on topics in customer service.
2. To read and analyze current customer service information.
3. To complete the current event form using good grammar and a professional writing style.

Assignment

Examine current business publications and/or the Internet to locate articles relating to current trends in customer service. Choose three articles that interest you and complete three separate current event forms. Read the articles and then answer the questions listed on the current event forms. Try to relate the information in your articles to what you have been learning as you have been studying customer service.

Presentation

Remove the current event form (Current Events and Customer Service). You will need to make copies or create your own form on the computer. Complete the forms in full. Try to be thorough yet concise as you answer each section. Use complete sentences and a professional writing style. The ability to read and understand current articles relating to business is a valuable skill that will serve you as you grow in professionalism.

ANSWERS TO QUICK QUIZ

1. F	5. F	9. F
2. F	6. F	10. T
3. T	7. F	
4. F	8. F	

Challenge
Current Events and
Customer Service

Name _____ Date _____

Name of article _____

Where did you find the article? (Name of the publication, include the web address if applicable) _____

What was the article about? (Give an overview of the article in your own words)

_____

_____

_____

_____

_____

_____

_____

_____

_____

What did you think about the article? (Include your opinions) _____

_____

_____

_____

Share any additional thoughts that you have about the article. _____

_____

_____

_____

Excellence in Customer Service

Remember This

Promises may get you friends, but it is performance that keeps them.

Owen Feltham

CHAPTER OBJECTIVES

In this chapter, you will learn how to

- Detail examples of active companies that are succeeding in the provision of outstanding customer service.

- Express the fundamental requirements of creating a successful customer service program.
- List the rewards of providing excellent customer service.

Excellence Is the Goal

To be successful in business today requires a commitment to excellence in customer service. If excellence is the goal, anything less is not acceptable. Many companies talk about the importance of providing excellent customer service and yet do little to initiate its offering. One of the most effective and least expensive ways to market a business is through the provision of excellent customer service. It is not really a question of whether or not a business wants to provide customer service to its customers. Every business must provide customer service, even if they do not really want to. It has become mandatory. Customer service is exciting! If every customer is seen as a valuable asset who is difficult to replace, they are more likely to be cherished. When talking to individuals who interact daily with customers, most will tell you that an extremely fulfilling part of their job is creating positive solutions for their customers. Happy customers keep coming back to do business and to renew the relationships that they have previously established.

What's Happening in the "Real World"?

Countless companies are providing outstanding customer service in the "real world" every day. Sometimes they go unnoticed because they make it so easy to do business with them. In all too many instances we, as customers, are just taking their services for granted. The following are profiles of a few of those outstanding companies that are all positive examples of customer service.

JKJ Benefits, LLC is an employee benefits/consulting firm in Fort Worth, Texas. They provide full-service employee benefits brokerage consulting in numerous states. JKJ strives to provide high-quality customer service with integrity.

JKJ considers service to be a defining difference in their business. They pursue an "old fashioned" approach to the ways in which they serve their customers. They call their customers instead of exclusively e-mailing them. Personal contact is vital as they service their customers' needs. That personal touch has allowed JKJ to hear customer successes and concerns, and to be proactive in addressing customer problems or new business opportunities.

Customers are actively reevaluating employee benefits based on cost. As they attempt to balance what they can afford to provide for their employees with how much the company can spend, insurance/benefits companies have a unique opportunity. JKJ is approaching this opportunity head-on. They learn their client's business so they can tailor the benefits offering to the unique characteristics of the clients. They then offer specialized continuing education options such as COBRA

(Consolidated Omnibus Budget Reconciliation Act) and FMLA (Family Medical Leave Act) and other customer programs to enhance their customers' ability to be successful in their respective businesses. JKJ sees partnering with customers as a beneficial marketing tool that has immeasurable payoffs for both the client's business and JKJ's.

JKJ is a young company but they clearly are striving to deliver excellence in customer service through a variety of opportunities and will be a company to watch in the years to come.

Quality Aircraft Accessories, Inc. (QAA) is a Class 1 and Class 2 FAA-approved repair station that overhauls, repairs, and exchanges aircraft engine accessories with customers primarily in the United States, but also in over 30 different countries. QAA is known in the general aviation industry for its one-day turn time when requested by customers. Parts that are shipped to QAA and received in the morning are repaired or overhauled and shipped back to the customer the same day whenever requested, and at no extra charge.

QAA has a very successful approach to customer satisfaction and retention. The management of this company consistently adheres to a policy of not leaving the office without resolving customer issues. This has had a very positive result in a world where one of many customers' greatest frustrations is not being contacted to resolve problems in a timely manner.

QAA rarely has a face-to-face interaction with their customers. This reality has compelled management to invest a lot of time training new employees to be professional, well informed, and excellent time managers as they take customer calls and orders. They do not use any type of automated phone system and therefore have determined optimal staffing and training to promptly assist their customers.

QAA knows that if their customers need a part or repair of a part, there is probably an aircraft on the ground that is not in the air doing its job. This realization has sped up the customer response time in contrast to competitors. QAA is not the highest price supplier in the market, but they are one of the higher ones. Customers receive numerous benefits from doing business with them though. QAA demonstrates professionalism in every thing they do.

In a non-face-to-face industry, packaging appearance says a tremendous amount about your company. With this in mind, QAA has established very strict and specific shipping requirements. All parts are shipped in specialized packing material that is not standard in the industry. The packing tape is printed with the company's logo and even the shipping label is customized and continues to enhance the company's image. QAA ships over 60 boxes each day and in five years has only had 3 UPS claims. This extremely low claim ratio caused UPS to honor the company as the cover story in the UPS publication *Compass* in the Winter 2007 premiere issue. High-quality packaging and shipping standards leave QAA customers with a positive final impression of their company and build on the established image of amazing customer service.

A final unique customer service strategy that QAA uses each year is to honor their top 100 customers. Because the customers they want to express appreciation to may not only work in the front office or in the shop, QAA looked for a unique "gift" to share with them. The perfect idea resulted in a local company that roasted peanuts. QAA ships 50–100 pound burlap bags of roasted peanuts to their valued customers. The customers hang the bags of peanuts in their shops and invite all of their employees from all areas to grab some peanuts and enjoy the appreciation gift. This unique tradition has become a much anticipated reward for important customers and goes a long way in successfully retaining their business. QAA is a success in customer service and a company that is an inspiration to learn more about.

An independent telecommunications company serves approximately 15,000 customers in Oklahoma providing a complete set of advanced communications services ranging from local service to broadband Internet and Ethernet transport. As a regulated utility, telephone companies are subject to the oversight of the Oklahoma Corporation Commission and must maintain a high level of customer service and customer communications. In its continuous attempt to keep pace with competitors and customers' ever-changing priorities, this company has recently introduced an updated website with a new look that offers new features to customers like online bill payment that even allows customers the option to pay by online check, savings, or credit cards. This allows customers to save on postage and takes away the need for many customers to physically come in to the office to make a payment. Ultimately, the company plans to utilize the Web to allow customers to self-provision services. Civic involvement is a defining quality of the telecommunications company. They regularly participate in sponsoring local festivals and celebrations. They are an active partner in their community and are viewed very positively by customers. A local customer service presence differentiates them from their competitors. Customers appreciate knowing that the voice on the phone is a friend and neighbor and that by doing business with the local telephone company, they are supporting their own business community.

Community colleges fulfill an important and unique niche of the higher education arena. A regional community college in the Midwest serving approximately 12,000+ students is on the cutting edge as they serve their growing student base. While the primary focus of any school is educating its students, academic institutions today face competition from a variety of other similar institutions and other opportunities that students may be motivated to pursue. Most community colleges have some type of an open-door policy which means that almost any student is eligible to enroll in school. After succeeding in attracting those students, numerous factors work together to successfully retain those students until they graduate or until they have achieved the goals that they have set for themselves.

Most colleges, including this one, are seeing a focus shift as they work to retain students. Students have a lot of concerns as they work to pursue educational goals. A concern that has always existed is that of being able to pay for tuition, fees, and books. In years past if a student could not pay these expenses before the start of a new semester, he or she probably did not get to attend. Obviously, a student that has to step out of school for a semester is at a huge risk of not returning. To address this concern, alternative payment methods have been created. Students now can pay upfront, monthly or on some other prearranged schedule. Financial aid is an increasingly important component of paying for school. By having financial aid advisors available to assist in the completion of paperwork, meeting of deadlines, and even having computers for applying for assistance in the financial aid area, students may be able to receive dollars that will allow them to fund their education. Since the timing of financial aid dollars may not coincide with the start of a term and the disbursement of checks is time consuming, this school, and many others, has adopted the use of a debit card system. In this type of system, every student has an account for financial aid disbursements and refunds. Automated teller machines (ATMs) are located across the campus so that students can pull out money or use it like a checking account. Overall, the coordination of financial aid and varying payment plans can assist significantly, removing one of the many concerns that students face.

Creating a seamless program for the transfer of classes to another school or university is another method for retaining students. University parallel programs allow students to automatically feed into degree programs at a university. Students know that they are taking a class that will transfer and will therefore expedite their degree completion. Developmental classes help students when courses are difficult or they are insufficiently prepared for the class in their prior education. Student success is an excellent method of retention in a learning setting. If a student can take a lower-level course to give them an appropriate understanding of the material, they can then be better prepared to succeed in a course that is a higher level that is required to complete their degree. High academic standards are stressed, and enabling students to be equipped to succeed keeps both external and internal customers happy and working together as a team.

The physical environment of this school is warm and inviting. The main classroom building feels a little like a mall setting. Parking is plentiful and once the students get into the building they usually stay on campus until they have completed their learning day. They can work and research in the well-appointed media center. Inviting spaces are located all across the campus. Group seating provides students a place to meet their friends or study groups or to just relax. The coffee bar is a fun place to hang out and to study. Retaining students is vital to the success of any educational system, but through the implementation of the diverse retention strategies students will be inspired to remain active customers in the process. Students are happy customers and sing the praises of this institution.

Most consumers take it for granted that when they flip a light switch the light will come on. When it doesn't who do we call? The electric company!

A large electric utility company in the South is an outstanding example of excellent customer service in action. With over 250 employees in the call center, billing, credit/collections, and related services, this utility must have the highest standards in hiring and training the proper people. A detailed screening process is the first step in identifying that appropriate person. Once they are identified as a potential candidate, they have a phone screening, then an interview with a panel of peers and supervisors, a behavioral test, and then if each of these steps goes well, they may receive a job offer. Once hired, the new employee has three months of training before they are allowed to take customer calls without a trainer's direction. This company sees a tremendous value in this detailed selection and training process. They currently have about a 6 percent turnover rate, and the majority of their employees plan to retire from the company.

All employees are trained to handle any call that comes in. They are empowered to address all customers' concerns from start to finish. They are trained to listen to what the customer may not be sharing that could be relevant to solving the customer's problems. Unique payment options and flexibility may be all that is necessary to help a customer handle a challenging circumstance. As the economic conditions are fluctuating, customers are more likely to request installment payments or may choose to use their credit card to pay their bill. New methods of serving external and internal customers are continually being explored. External customers are offered different billing options, customer information, and superior service. Internal customers are offered unique work opportunities, career pathing, and job shadowing to identify areas they may want to pursue for promotions within the company and a very attractive and fun work environment.

During a catastrophic ice storm a few years ago, customers really saw this company's dedication to their customers in action. With up to 75 percent of their customers suffering from power outages due to the ice, these employees still came in to work to answer customer calls. The same employees were in many cases also without power at their homes. With temperatures in the teens for several days, customer tensions were very high. People were cold and sitting in the dark. They wanted their power back on NOW! Customer calls were handled with professionalism and patience while at the same time repair crews from all over the country were outside in the cold working to get the power back on. The electric company recruited players from the area football teams to assist in checking on older customers and completing basic paperwork. Some customers were able to restore power within a few days; some others were without power for several weeks. When power was restored, customer feedback was very positive. It was a difficult circumstance that was made better by a provider that had employees that wanted to do all that they could to assist their customers.

The examples of excellence in customer service are abundant. Pay attention to those providers that service you faithfully. We can all learn something from their example.

Getting Started

Unfortunately, the main reason that more businesses are just talking about the importance of customer service and are not actually providing it is because they do not know how to get started. After reading this selecttion and working through the skill-building exercises and challenges, you have explored the fundamental requirements of creating a successful customer service program. You now know much more than the average customer service provider or customer service manager. Take the knowledge that you have acquired and begin to offer your customers an enhanced customer experience.

Rewards of Providing Excellent Customer Service

Companies that provide excellent customer service experience many rewards. Ten of the most beneficial follow:

1. Customers approach business expecting a positive experience.
2. Work is more personally fulfilling.
3. Customers act as coproducers (when appropriate) in assisting in the provision of their own customer service.
4. A unique competitive edge is achieved.
5. Customer challenges are recognized and productive solutions are developed to successfully retain current customers.
6. Problems are creatively solved in an effective and efficient manner.
7. Customer service providers and management feel positive about the roles that they are playing in creating positive exchanges between customers and their organization.
8. Work environments are more pleasant and productive because the value of internal customers is stressed through organization policies, procedures, and culture.
9. Businesses earn a positive reputation and the respect of customers and peers.
10. Profit goals are more successfully accomplished because business philosophies and focus are on satisfying customers.

The challenge of seeking and achieving excellence in customer service is not easily overcome. Equipped with the knowledge necessary to create an environment that encourages excellent customer service, and the skills to successfully compete in the industry, the next step is to embark on the path of achieving individual and organizational excellence in customer service.

Index